Boko Haram and the Drivers of Islamist Violence

This book analyzes the factors that drive Boko Haram's violence, arguing that the movement is rooted in the historical and religious context of west Africa.

The data presented is based on extensive research, including fieldwork in Nigeria, primary source analysis, archival work, and large-scale survey analyses. Each chapter deals with a different case-study that showcases a driver of Boko Haram's violence, including how the jihad of Usman dan Fodio is used as a source of contemporary inspiration to Boko Haram; how the extrajudicial killing of its then leader Mohammad Yusuf spurred the group to violence; why the kidnapping of the Chibok schoolgirls was motivated by both ideology and strategy; how the formation of a caliphate and pledging of allegiance to ISIS gave Boko Haram an amplified presence; and how the issue of *takfir* led to the fracturing of the movement. To succeed in the fight against Boko Haram, this book argues, the Nigerian state needs to couple military advances with deep social changes, such as combatting corruption, reforming the police, and investing equitably across the country.

This book will be of much interest to students of terrorism and political violence, African politics, war and conflict studies, and security studies in general.

Zacharias P. Pieri is a political sociologist at the University of South Florida, USA.

Boko Haram and the Drivers of Islamist Violence

Zacharias P. Pieri

Routledge
Taylor & Francis Group

LONDON AND NEW YORK

First published in paperback 2024

First published 2019
by Routledge
4 Park Square, Milton Park, Abingdon, Oxon OX14 4RN

and by Routledge
605 Third Avenue, New York, NY 10158

Routledge is an imprint of the Taylor & Francis Group, an informa business

Publisher's Note
The publisher has gone to great lengths to ensure the quality of this reprint but
points out that some imperfections in the original copies may be apparent.

British Library Cataloguing-in-Publication Data
A catalogue record for this book is available from the British Library

Library of Congress Cataloging-in-Publication Data
A catalog record has been requested for this book

ISBN: 978-1-138-61186-3 (hbk)
ISBN: 978-1-03-293076-3 (pbk)
ISBN: 978-0-429-46517-8 (ebk)

DOI: 10.4324/9780429465178

Typeset in Times New Roman
by Apex CoVantage, LLC

Contents

Acknowledgements

This book is the culmination of seven years of research on Boko Haram that started with a project examining the drivers of violence in west Africa, at the University of South Florida. During this time, I benefitted from numerous collaborations, conversations, and exchanges of ideas with colleagues including David Jacobson, Natalie Deckard, Rafael Serrano, and Atta Barkindo. Research for this book spanned across three continents including Africa, Europe, and the United States. In Nigeria I was privileged to access archival materials in Ibadan as well as Abuja, and was assisted by the knowledgeable librarians and archivists who also helped me navigate Nigeria more broadly. In the United Kingdom I accessed materials at the British Library, the National Archives at Kew Gardens, and the Bodleian Library's Commonwealth and African Manuscripts Archives. In each instance plentiful assistance made my task of identifying and accessing documents a pleasurable experience. In the United States, Daniel Reboussin, Head of the African Studies Collections at the University of Florida, allowed free access to the papers of Ronald Cohen.

I am very grateful to have benefitted from engaging conversations and collaboration with Jacob Zenn on all aspects of Boko Haram, and who also provided critique and feedback on the chapters dealing with Boko Haram's acquisition of territory and the movement's fracturing. Likewise, I am appreciative of Elizabeth Pearson and Cassie Yacovazzi, both of whom gave generously of their time to review draft chapters. Jane Clark edited the manuscript with meticulous attention to detail, expertly correcting grammatical and syntactical errors as well as making suggestions for improvement. I am especially appreciative of Sandy Justice, Senior Research Administrator at the University of South Florida Sarasota-Manatee, who was supportive of this book from the very beginning. Helene Robinson's writing retreat at USFSM fostered an atmosphere of creative productivity and encouraged the writing process.

I am indebted to Andrew Humphreys, Senior Editor for Military, Strategic, and Security Studies at Routledge, who has carefully managed this process; Bethany Lund-Yates, who kept me on schedule; and Hannah Ferguson, who first approached me about writing a book on this topic.

I would be remiss not to thank my family for their continued support – my parents Peter and Katerina, and my grandmother Margarita, who has always encouraged me to pursue my interests and to never give up. Thanks are also due to Elaine M. Goodwin, Michael Williams, Samantha Haylock, Landon Rutledge, Lucrezia Coco, and Cobalt Cristian. My deepest gratitude is reserved for my Nigerian participants as well as the people of northern Nigeria, many of whom have suffered as a result of the brutal conflict. Any errors are of course my own.

Abbreviations

AQIM	Al Qaeda in the Islamic Maghreb
IDPs	Internally Displaced Persons
ISWAP	Islamic State West Africa Province
JAS	Jamaat Ahl as Sunnah Lid dawa wa al-Jihad
LCB	Lake Chad Basin
RPGs	Rocket-Propelled Grenades
NGOs	Non-Governmental Organizations
VOA	Voice of America

Specialized terms

Amir	leader/ruler
boko	sham/fraud (often applied to western culture)
chadour	cloak-like garment
dar al-Islam	abode of Islam
da'wa	propagation of Islam
haad	punishments mandated under Islamic law
haram	forbidden
hijra	migration
hisbah	accountability
kafir	infidel
mai	king
majlis	consultative body
niqab	veil covering the face
shalwar-kemeez	long shirt and baggy pants
shari'a	Islamic law
taghut	worship other that Allah
takfir	act of excommunication
tafsir	exegesis

1 Introduction

Setting the scene

Before 2014, Boko Haram was – at least to most in the west – a little known Islamist group. The movement was situated in northeastern Nigeria, with operational capacity extending into the sparsely governed lands around the Lake Chad Basin (LCB) at the intersection of the borders of Nigeria, Chad, Niger, and Cameroon. Brutally violent since resurfacing in 2011, after the extrajudicial killing of its then leader Mohammad Yusuf in 2009, Boko Haram gained the reputation of attacking all those opposed to its activities and was designated a Foreign Terrorist Organization by the United States in 2013.[1] It was not until the Spring of 2014, under the leadership of Abubakar Shekau, that the group occupied international headlines. It was the kidnapping of 276 school girls from their dormitories at the Government Girls Secondary School in Chibok, the night before the girls' final exams, that brought Boko Haram to global notoriety. Images of distraught parents crying, juxtaposed with Shekau promising to convert the girls to Islam or sell them into 'slavery' (Shekau 2014), reverberated across the world. In quick succession to this, Boko Haram acquired territory in northeastern Nigeria, announced the creation of a so-called Islamic state there, and pledged allegiance to Abu Bakar al-Baghdadi's Islamic State (in Iraq and Syria). With this pledge, Boko Haram's name changed to Islamic State West Africa Province (ISWAP), initiating Boko Haram as a formal franchise of the Islamic State.

There has been a dramatic increase in media reporting on Boko Haram, with fears of the movement forming deeper links with international jihadist organizations. Consequently, there has been a clamor for more insight and analysis. It is upon this increase in awareness and the need to understand Boko Haram – what it is, where it stems from, how it recruits and operates, and how it can be challenged – that this book is based. It will provide an analysis of Boko Haram and the broader conflict in Nigeria and west Africa, and is propelled by the desire to identify and analyze the drivers of Boko Haram's violence.

In order to understand these drivers of violence, this book places Boko Haram in the historical, religious, socio-political, and cultural context of Nigeria and the LCB. The argument is that Boko Haram cannot be understood in a vacuum but rather must be seen as a product of different factors that have festered in the region, in some cases, over hundreds of years. As such, the book identifies a number of drivers of Boko Haram's violence, including the historical (how Boko Haram leaders have interpreted and reframed the Islamic history of the region), contextual (issues around state corruption, political disenfranchisement of the northeast, and state brutality), and ideological (Salafi-jihadism, *takfirism*, and animosity to western education and culture). It also looks at the evolving dynamics of Boko Haram, including the fracturing of the movement and competition between the different branches, and possible desires for links with other more internationally oriented jihadist movements. Added to this are the more individual drivers of violence – that is, the factors considering why people joined Boko Haram, why they remained in the movement, and why they have been willing to kill on its behalf. These include what Boko Haram has to offer – money, weapons, brides, notions of hyper-masculinity, and even a sense of community. Revenge against the state also motivates some, while others truly believe in the vision of the movement.

It was questionable as to whether Boko Haram at its foundation in the early 2000s would become violent, though there was violent imagery in its discourse even from this period. While its then leader Mohammad Yusuf talked about the 19th-century Islamic reformer Usman Dan Fodio and his jihad in 1804 that overthrew the Hausa states to create the Sokoto Caliphate as being admirable, Boko Haram's initial emphasis was on addressing social grievances. These grievances centered around state corruption, nepotism, failure to properly implement *shari'a* law, and the brutalizing of the population at the hands of the police. Boko Haram stood at the apex of providing a voice of opposition to the incompetence of the Nigerian state. Mohammad Yusuf was adept at framing the solution to social ills and grievances through his own Salafist interpretation of Islam. The use of Islam as a resonant framework for combating social ills is nothing new, and indeed has a long history not only in west Africa but also with other Islamist movements (both non-violent and violent) such as Tablighi Jamaat, the Muslim Brotherhood, and Al Qaeda.

While a number of volumes have now been written on Boko Haram (Perouse de Montclos 2014; Mustapha 2014; Comolli 2015; Walker 2016; Varin 2016; Hentz & Solomon 2017; Thurston 2018; Zenn 2018; Kassim & Nwankpa 2018), the fast-paced and changing dynamics of the realities on the ground mean that new information about the movement, the way it operates, and its path of evolution are still emerging. This book will provide analysis of Boko Haram that complements much of what has already been written while making unique contributions to the understanding of the drivers of Boko Haram violence, especially with regards to the ways in which the forces of history have propelled the movement, how its extremist ideology led to changing relationships with other Islamist actors and ultimately to Boko Haram's own fracturing, and the ways in which it attempted (at least for a short time) to balance violence with governance in the territories it seized into its "Islamic state."

Mustapha (2014: 166) identifies five pillars for analyzing Boko Haram's actions and lists them as '1) religious doctrines, 2) poverty and inequality – vertical and horizontal, 3) the political context of post-1999 electoral competition, 4) the personal agency of the youth directly involved in Boko Haram, and 5) the geographical and international context of the insurgency.' To this, Thurston (2018: 5) adds the importance of politics in the sense that 'jihadist movements are actors, and in the additional sense that political developments can enable or constrain their activities.' While useful in providing a multidimensional approach to understanding Boko Haram, such a framework can, in Thurston's (2018: 5) opinion, act as a ' "kitchen sink" problem where anything and everything is proposed as an explanation for Boko Haram.' In order to avoid this, my approach is to emphasize how Boko Haram's interpretation of history fused with contextual issues around poor governance and Salafist ideology to create a lethal situation.

Contested name

While "Boko Haram" will be used throughout the book to refer to the movement, it is not a name officially accepted for it by its leaders. The name has stuck, and because of this, it is important to consider the meaning behind it, as well as to discuss other names that the movement selected for itself. "Boko Haram" is often popularly (mis)translated as "Western education is forbidden" on the assumption that *Boko* is taken from the English word meaning book, and *Haram* from the Arabic word meaning forbidden (Newman 2013: 2). While this encapsulates one element of the group's ideology (its stance against non-Islamic teachings), it is a name that the movement has rejected. The name constricts our understanding of what Boko Haram is by endorsing a monolithic view of Boko Haram as anti-education when, actually, the movement represents doctrines and actions that extend well beyond education. The more authentic translation of the word *Boko* ironically comes closer to the way in which Boko Haram leaders imagine the movement. According to Paul Newman (2013: 8), *Boko* originally meant

'Something (an idea or object) that involves a fraud or any form of deception' and, by extension, the noun denoted 'any reading or writing which is not connected with Islam.' Indeed, as early as Boko Haram's re-formation in August 2009 as a self-avowed jihadist group, Abubakar Shekau (2009), the then leader, said 'Western education is part of a broader civilizational project to detach Muslims from Islam and its Arabic language traditions, and instead immerse Muslims in Christianity and English-language.' Thus, opposition to Western education is but one ingredient in a much broader construction of Boko Haram's ideology. This is nowhere better captured than in a statement by Sanni Umar, a brief successor to Mohammad Yusuf, in August 2009:

> Boko Haram does not in any way mean "western education is a sin" as the infidel media continue to portray us. Boko Haram actually means "western civilization" is forbidden. The difference is that while the first gives the impression that we are opposed to formal education coming from the west, that is Europe, which is not true, the second affirms our belief in the supremacy of Islamic culture (not education), for culture is broader; it includes education but not determined by western education. In this case we are talking of western ways of life which include: constitutional provision as it relates to, for instance, the rights and privileges of women, the idea of homosexualism, lesbianism, multi-party democracy in an overwhelmingly Islamic country like Nigeria, blue films, prostitution, drinking beer and alcohol and many others that are opposed to Islamic civilization.[2]

In 2009, Boko Haram leaders started to refer to their movement as *Jamaat Ahl as Sunnah Lid dawa wa al-Jihad* (Sunni Group for Proselytization and Jihad), or JAS, and published a series of communiques explaining that they believed themselves to be distinct Muslims. The impact of this was that those who did not join JAS, including "mainstream" Muslims and even those following a Salafist strand of Islam but who were considered to have "sold out" to the Nigerian state, are not part of *Ahl as Sunnah* (Zenn & Pieri 2017: 282). Instead, all those falling outside of what Boko Haram defined as a pure Muslim were classified as *kafir* or infidels. Such extreme actions, while not completely unprecedented in Islam, are nevertheless controversial. This was reflected even within the ranks of Boko Haram, with some key leaders rejecting this line of reasoning, eventually contributing to the fracturing of the movement.

In August 2014, Shekau made a pledge of allegiance to Abu Bakar al-Baghdadi's Islamic State. When the pledge was accepted by the Islamic State, Boko Haram changed its name from JAS to Islamic State West Africa

Province (ISWAP). The name change demonstrated a new direction for Boko Haram, namely to follow the ideologies of the Islamic State and to represent it in west Africa, meaning an expansion in its activities beyond Nigeria and the LCB – though this did not come to fruition. Due to continued disagreements in the movement over the doctrine of *takfir* – the permissibility to excommunicate Muslims, thus making them legitimate targets for killing – Boko Haram fractured. Shekau's literalist and unbending approach to *takfir* resulted in his demotion by the Islamic State from being the emir of ISWAP and spurred Shekau into re-banding under the formerly defunct name of JAS. As such there are now two distinct groups in Nigeria which are referred to as Boko Haram: ISWAP, which is officially affiliated to the Islamic State and takes a more moderate stance to *takfir*; and JAS, led by Shekau, which is not formally affiliated to the Islamic State and takes a literalist approach to *takfir*.

A note on sources

Given that Boko Haram is a violent jihadist organization which stands firmly opposed to any form of western education, it should come as no surprise my time was not spent with the movement, nor indeed in northeastern Nigeria. In order to mitigate that, my research time in Nigeria was spent in other parts of the country, particularly in the north, including Abuja and Kano. While in Nigeria I met with and interviewed people affected by Boko Haram's violence in the northeast and with people who had direct experience of the movement. Internally Displaced Persons (IDPs) fleeing from the northeast were able to provide valuable insight as to what was happening in Borno State at the height of Boko Haram's power, while interviews with government officials, military officers, and NGOs, all working on the ground, were able to add further perceptions. Excerpts from interviews are used throughout the book, though any names mentioned are pseudonyms in order to protect the participants unless the comments made were a matter of public record.

The book draws on statements and videos released by Boko Haram. Such materials are regarded as propaganda and are treated in a critical manner, while at the same time recognizing the value they bring to understanding the publicly expressed ideologies of the movement and, at times, its internal dynamics and relationship with other jihadist entities. Over the course of seven years of research on Boko Haram, approximately 100 items of primary source materials, including press statements, sermons, pamphlets, speeches, and videos, were collected. Many of these, up until Shekau's response to his critics on December 18, 2016, have since been collated and published in a useful primary source reader, *The Boko Haram Reader:*

From Nigerian Preachers to the Islamic State by Kassim and Nwankpa (2018), and for the sake of ease, material that was used and available in this reader will be attributed to that. All other primary sources will be referenced to the original source.

Three additional primary sources stand out as being of particular value and importance to this book. The first is a cache of videos taken from the hard drives of Boko Haram laptops and released in 2017 by Voice of America (VOA). The footage shows an unparalleled look into how Boko Haram attempted to govern territories seized in 2014. Given that these videos were shot for internal purposes and not for propaganda, they present a unique picture of the movement at the zenith of its power. The second source is a book released by the ISWAP faction of Boko Haram, *Slicing the Tumor*, purportedly written by two sons of former leader Mohammad Yusuf and which presents a history of Boko Haram as well as an attempt to delegitimize Shekau as an extremist. While clearly biased, the document is important for shedding light on the origins of Boko Haram, how and why the dispute over *takfir* arose, and the internal dynamics of the movement. The third source is a survey completed by Gallup in Nigeria from 2013. The face-to-face survey included both open- and close-ended questions and was completed by 10,482 Nigerian residents from every region of the country. Though much has changed in Nigeria since 2013, the data provides a snapshot of attitudes at the juncture when Boko Haram transformed into a violent organization and is thus very important in helping us to understand how the movement evolved over time.

In addition to this, the book draws on a range of historical sources dealing with the pre-colonial, colonial, and immediate post-colonial periods in Nigeria. Of importance were documents pertaining to the jihad of Usman dan Fodio, the complete archives of Lord Fredrick Lugard (the first Governor of Nigeria) which deal with British colonial policy in Nigeria, Nigerian archives on the post-colonial period, and the Ronald Cohen archives based at the University of Florida, which provide an ethnographic snapshot of Bono and the Kanuri in the immediate post-colonial period.

Layout of the book

Following this introduction, Chapter 2 will contextualize Boko Haram within a history of jihad and Islamic violence in Nigeria. The chapter argues that Boko Haram is the product of a long historical process of which it is only the latest iteration. This is something Boko Haram is attuned to. Movement leaders have an entrenched knowledge of Nigerian and Islamic history; of the Kanem-Borno Empire which once ruled huge portions of west Africa from its capital in northeastern Nigeria; of the jihad of Usman

Dan Fodio in 1804 which swept away the Hausa states of north(western) Nigeria and ushered in the Sokoto Caliphate (Last 1967; Suliman 2009); and increasingly of deterritorialized and decontextualized Islam preached by Salafi jihadists as the solution to the ills of the world. Boko Haram leaders have been skillful at drawing upon, interpreting, and misinterpreting history to show people in northern Nigeria that the movement is part of a legitimate procession of movements that have had to use violent means in order to usher in a more Islamically compliant social order. To this extent, Boko Haram leaders have been adept in using historical narratives to drive a violent agenda.

Chapter 3 argues that Boko Haram must be analyzed in conjunction with prescient contemporary socio-political factors at work in Nigeria, including rampant corruption (Deckard & Pieri 2016), immeasurable police and military brutality (Serano & Pieri 2014), a sense of disenfranchisement in northern Nigeria, and the reassertion of Islam as a primary identity. It was the fusion of these contextual factors with Boko Haram's interpretation of history that provided the initial impetus for violent mobilization against the state. Based on survey data and interviews in Nigeria, the chapter shows low levels of affinity with the Nigerian federal government for those living in the northeast and little trust in public institutions, including the police and military. These factors allowed Mohammad Yusuf to formulate concrete grievances against the state and spurred him to create a parallel society with his own schools, medical clinics, and newspaper outside of the state's jurisdiction. Islam was framed as the solution to all social and political problems in Nigeria. This chapter captures Boko Haram initially as a social movement and charts its progress to violence after 2009 when Yusuf was extrajudicially killed by the security services. Further discussed are factors that drove individuals to violence on behalf of Boko Haram and issues around recruitment and mobilization of members.

Chapter 4 focuses on ideology as a driver of Boko Haram's violence. The popular translation of Boko Haram as "Western education is sin" does not encapsulate everything the movement stands for, though this has been a big part of its *raison d'etre*. Both Yusuf and Shekau showed deep distain for western learning, attributing all things evil to it. Boko Haram members initially burned degree certificates, then attacked schools and killed teachers. Perhaps the most infamous action was the kidnapping of hundreds of schoolgirls in Chibok and beyond. The chapter will trace why Boko Haram took the schoolgirls, what happened to them, and how education remains central to Boko Haram's violence. From Boko Haram's perspective the girls were not kidnapped, but rather liberated, and many of the released videos of the girls from Boko Haram show them being "re-educated" by the movement.

Boko Haram's long-term stated goal was the dismantling of the Nigerian state which they viewed as an aberration of history, an illegitimate colonial construct, and putting in its place the establishment of territory ruled under *shari'a* law. While Boko Haram was not able to achieve this goal in its totality, it was able, for a short period of time, to establish territory in the three northeastern states of Nigeria. Chapter 5 demonstrates that the fusion of historical interpretation with a desire for territorial acquisition functioned as a driver of Boko Haram's violence. The chapter will show how Boko Haram mobilized operationally and strategically to seize territory and to declare an Islamic entity that has 'nothing to do with the state of Nigeria' (Shekau 2014). The chapter argues that the re-integration of a Boko Haram splinter group, with close ties to Al Qaeda in the Islamic Magherb (AQIM), back into Boko Haram provided the technical know-how and strategic expertise Boko Haram needed to conquer territory. Internal Boko Haram footage from Boko Haram will show how it attempted to govern in the areas it briefly controlled.

Chapter 6 examines Boko Haram's factionalization through the lens of the doctrine of *takfir* – how it has been interpreted and implemented by different leaders in Boko Haram and how excessive violence against the Muslim civilian population led the movement to split. The years between 2014 and 2015 saw a peak in Boko Haram's power, when the movement held large portions of land, thousands of captives and resources, and a formal relationship with Islamic State. Though, as of early 2019, Boko Haram factions are still able to launch large-scale attacks in northeastern Nigeria, its territorial holdings have been extinguished, and its leadership has fractured. The chapter considers the consequences of this fracturing on the evolution of the movement, its relationships with the wider international jihadist scene, and its continued ability to wage war against the Nigerian state.

The book concludes by arguing that even if the Nigerian state were to defeat Boko Haram militarily, the drivers of Islamist violence in Nigeria also need to be combated. This demands a response that goes beyond a military effort and requires a painful rethinking of Nigerian historical narratives, especially over the widely celebrated caliphate of Usman dan Fodio. The Nigerian state has to learn that the drivers of Islamist violence are deeply intertwined with issues around state corruption, state brutality, and a failure of the state to implement policies that benefit all Nigerian citizens. Until these are addressed in meaningful ways, it is likely that there will be more Islamist groups promising solutions to the ills of Nigeria based on a utopian version of Islam – though given the experience with Boko Haram, how willing a population is to believe these is a different matter.

Notes

1 See list of Foreign Terrorist Organizations, U.S. Department of State. www.state.
   gov/j/ct/rls/other/des/123085.htm (accessed: May 31, 2018).
2 Umar, S. 2009. 'Statement of Sani Umaru', in Kassim, A. and Nwankpa, M. (eds.).
   The Boko Haram Reader: From Nigerian Preachers to the Islamic State. Oxford:
   Oxford University Press, pp. 207–208.

2 On the Islamic history of Nigeria

Introduction

The lessons of history have been of central importance to Boko Haram's leaders, who look to the past to see how Islamic empires in west Africa were destroyed by weak-willed leaders who failed to rule in strict accordance with *shari'a* law and by ruthless European colonial regimes that carved up the continent in order to divide Muslims and keep them subjugated. For Boko Haram's leaders, it does not have to be this way; there is a rejection that this is the natural course of history, and instead they see it as an aberration. In history, Boko Haram leaders see a vision of the future – one that is mirrored on pre-colonial forms of governance – and one they have demonstrated a willingness for violence to achieve. Mohammad Yusuf (d. 2009), a foundational leader of Boko Haram, often highlighted historical injustice in his sermons and believed that only a return to strict Islamic governance could rectify the sorry state of affairs in northern Nigeria and the wider Lake Chad Basin (LCB):

> Europe designed various strategies of subjugation. Islamic countries were realigned based on the availability of mineral resources and all this was the wisdom of the European countries. For example, northern Niger and northern Nigeria were actually one Islamic country with no difference between the two.[1]

In the same sermon he would go on to say:

> They amalgamated us [northern Nigeria] to infidels and unbelievers. Then they left Niger on their own, knowing that Niger is very poor and poverty will pose no threat. As of Chad, Europeans created ethnic problems, amalgamated them to other infidels and unbelievers and established a rotational system of political authority between the tribes. This

led to political instability in Chad since the time of Tumbal Mai[2] and as a result, the country has remained inseparable from conflict. In the case of Sudan, the country was forcefully amalgamated with south Sudan.[3]

Yusuf's sermons show that he did not recognize the sovereignty of the Nigerian state. Instead he saw the state as an illegitimate construct brought into being by European colonialism, with the intent of dividing the Muslim populations of the region. The repudiation of constitutional democracy, which is viewed as part of the colonial project in Nigeria, is key to Boko Haram's objectives. It also argues that Muslim leaders during the colonial period failed to protect the population from western influences, a charge that it also levels against Muslim leaders in Nigeria today. Boko Haram's ire is directed as much against Muslim leaders who fail to live up to the strictest standards of Islamic orthodoxy as it is to rectifying these historical injustices. While the call to jihad as a means of overturning these injustices, as well as the establishment of Islamic territory in the region, would not come until a later date, the framework to do so was in place from the movement's foundations. History for Boko Haram shows clear images of successful empires that were ruled under *shari'a* law, such as the Kanem-Borno Empire (700–1893 AD) and the Caliphate of Sokoto (1804–1903 AD), and so, for Boko Haram, no other system of governance is acceptable.

The aim of this chapter is simple – it is to show that Boko Haram cannot be understood without first comprehending the context, both distant and immediate, from which it emerged, and to show that the way in which Boko Haram views history is important to understanding its motivations and actions. The context, however, is complex. It predates the creation of the nation-state of Nigeria and stretches at its furthest point back to the establishment of the Kanem-Borno Empire and the arrival of Islam to the region in the 9th century AD. Kanem-Borno would come to dominate vast stretches of west Africa, including parts of what are now northeastern Nigeria, northwestern Chad, northern Cameroon, and southeastern Niger. While some scholars explain the emergence of Boko Haram as a result of the Nigerian state's inability to meet its statutory obligations to its citizens (Aghedo 2017), this chapter places the movement within northern Nigeria's historical trajectory of Islamic empires and jihads. Boko Haram cannot be understood in a vacuum, nor as a rogue Islamist movement bent on toppling the Nigerian state simply because of the shortfallings of the post-colonial state, but rather as part of a longer tradition of revolutionary Islamist movements that came before it. These movements which inspire Boko Haram fashioned northern Nigeria into what it is today and provide detail on how to usher in an Islamic state. In this sense Boko Haram is in keeping with other Islamist groups – looking back at some glorious past and projecting that template on present difficulties.

During the late 18th and early 19th centuries a number of reformist movements arose almost simultaneously throughout Muslim lands with the aim of restoring the Muslim world to what they believed was its former greatness. These movements called for a reorientation of whole societies to the highest ideals of Islam – in essence a return to the foundations of the religion as practiced by the prophet Mohammad and his companions. The most important of these movements was the Wahhabis of Arabia at the end of the 18th century, but perhaps more significant to west Africa were the three jihads of western Sudan of the 19th century led respectively by Usman dan Fodio (d. 1817), Seku Amadu Bari (d. 1845), and al-Haji Umar (d. 1864). These movements arose across vast geographic regions, some inspired by Sufi principles and others by more orthodox thought – they all shared, however, a belief in the reform and purification of Islam.[4] This implied the attempt to restore the original model of the Islamic state, as it was believed to have existed in the time of Mohammad and the first four generations of Muslims that followed him: 'a state in which social justice, administrated in the light of the *shari'a* by God fearing rulers, took the place of the arbitrary decisions of irresponsible and effectively non-Muslim despots' (Crowder 1962: 83).

The movements that emerged at the time were complex and fused together different strands of Islamic thought, often encompassing aspects from both Sufi mysticism and puristic orthodoxy simultaneously (Brenner 1979: 161). The most important of these movements in the case of the Nigerian context today is that of Usman dan Fodio. The impact of dan Fodio's teachings and subsequent jihad in Hausaland was transformative, serving to establish the Sokoto Caliphate, which dominated the governance structure of most of what is now northern Nigeria, into the British phase of colonialism. Boko Haram's demands, on the surface at least, differ little from those originally made by dan Fodio and the other reformers – namely the end of corruption by elites, the curbing of immorality and public sin, and a return to a way of life governed by the *shari'a*.

Yet, there is a paradox at play here. While Boko Haram is seeking to create its Islamic state based on the revivalist ideology of dan Fodio, its expansion is almost fully within the boundaries of the historic Kanem-Borno Empire, which is the traditional homeland of the Kanuri. Not only were the two empires (Kanem-Borno and Sokoto) not on the best of terms, but the way Islam was practiced in Borno differed significantly. This is well captured in observations made by the German explorer Dr. A. Schultze (1913: 171), who noted that the ordinances of the Kanuri are 'very laxly observed, as is shown especially by the very slightly secluded life of the extremely coquettish Kanuri lady, who is thus enabled to play a definite part in public life, and who even apart from this shows none of the reserve of her sisters in strict Mohammaden countries.' Dan Fodio's heartland of Sokoto, in which a stricter interpretation of Islam was implemented, has today remained largely outside of Boko Haram's orbit. This represents the main paradox of Boko Haram: 'it seeks legitimacy and inspiration from dan Fodio, the Fulani founder of the Sokoto Caliphate, in order to create its own caliphate, but its leaders and members are predominantly Kanuri operating in the areas of the former Kanuri-led Kanem-Borno Empire' (Pieri & Zenn 2016: 68).

Reviving an Islamic state in the west African context is important to Boko Haram and has functioned as one of the main drivers of the movement's violence. The Kanuri ethnicity of Boko Haram leaders, and the desire to see their homelands converting to Islamic systems of governance, explains why Boko Haram focused on Kanuri heartlands, but it is the way in which Boko Haram leaders manipulated the Islamic history of the region that can explain why they were successful in that initial drive. Boko Haram manipulates and reconciles the history and identities of northwestern and northeastern Nigeria to advance its goal of creating a caliphate based on dan Fodio's "northwestern model," but in the ethnic heartlands of the Kanuri in northeastern Nigeria. The chapter will provide an account of the Sokoto jihad, arguing that many of the same grievance factors that spurred the 1804 jihad were identified by members of Boko Haram as existing in contemporary Nigeria and used to drive its own jihad. The leaders of Boko Haram have been adroit, much like dan Fodio, in identifying local grievances – corruption, nepotism, a failure to implement *shari'a* – and merged these with a powerful Islamic discourse that preaches active change, even if that change is achieved through violence. The 19th century jihad served to dramatically change the landscape of northern Nigeria – implementing a system under which people were governed through the *shari'a* and on which daily interactions were molded by Islamic principles. For many in northern Nigeria, the system implemented by dan Fodio resonates to this day. It is seen as a system that is superior to the divisive politics of so-called democratic rule and as a solution to the ills of society. Therefore, in order to understand Boko Haram, a history of the Islamic landscape of Nigeria is needed.

The currents of history

Nigeria as a modern nation-state was created in 1914 under British colonial rule through the amalgamation of the Northern Protectorate of Nigeria, the Southern Protectorate of Nigeria, and the Colony of Lagos (Falola &

Heaton 2008: 117). It is an irredentist state, includes a plethora of ethnicities and identities, and is increasingly divided along religious lines – Islam and Christianity. Nigeria's north has enjoyed a long relationship with Islam. Islam first entered the region in the 9th century through the Kanem-Borno Empire – the historic lands of the Kanuri people, a people that now form a majority of the inhabitants of Nigeria's northeastern provinces and who spill over into the neighboring countries of Niger, Chad, and Cameroon (Alkali 1985: 127). This is also the area in which Boko Haram originated and where it has maintained its operational stronghold. Kanuri records claim that by the 11th century Islam was firmly established in the kingdom and that they and their leaders have been taking part in the annual Hajj since that time. Records speak of a Kanuri *Mai* – or king – Mai Hume ibn Abduljalil, who is reported to have died in Egypt on his way to Mecca, and that later his son, Mai Dunoma Humeni, undertook the pilgrimage on four occasions (Cohen 1967: 14). The implication of this is that the rulers of Kanem, having accepted Islam, took the religion seriously, while also reinforcing in the modern period that Borno has deep roots in Islamic governance. For movements such as Boko Haram, it is a selective reading of history – with Borno presented as a land with a long history of Islamic governance and, as such, needing to return to Islamic rule today. The historical record (Cohen 1967; Schultze 1913), however, also shows that the implementation of Islam in Borno was lax, that there was a plethora of thriving non-Muslim peoples, and that it was not colonialism that led to the decline of the empire but rather internal administrative disorganization and military attacks from neighboring powers.

By the 12th and 13th centuries Kanem-Borno had become a well-known state in the Islamic world. Islam continued to spread, though not always east from Borno, but north from Sudan, reaching Hausaland and the city of Kano (west of Borno), according to the Kano Chronicle, in the 14th century (Danmole 1996: 210). Initially a religion for rulers and elites, Islam filtered down to the wider population, although a blend of Islamic and non-Islamic practices remained in co-existence for centuries. British colonial records from 1949 reinforce this, with C.R. Niven (1949), Resident at Maiduguri, noting that:

> The Shehu of Bornu is the Kaliph of the East. Both Darfur and Fashr in Sudan recognize the religious suzerainty of the Shehu. The Kanuri are religious Orthodox Mohammedans. Two thirds of the population of the province are Kanuri and one third consists of various other tribes. The population of the province is 1,750,000 of which 60% are Kanuri and 20% are Shuwa Arab. The Fulani have never really been counted properly . . . There are a great many pagans across the south of the province, these are non-Muslim animists. A large number of the so-called

Muslims have a foot in both camps, i.e. they will indulge in sacrifices, etc. and their Muslimism is not of a very profound order. There are about 10,000 Christians in the province.

To the west of Kanem-Borno, by the beginning of the 19th century, the majority of rulers in Hausaland – the Habe as they were known – were Muslim, though Islam was not always practiced in accordance with the principles and ideals of the religion (Danmole 1996: 210). As far as the Habe monarchs were concerned, they practiced a calculated syncretism. This meant that while they identified themselves as Muslim and often ruled through Islamic systems of governance, their authority as rulers also had to be boosted via other means. The Habe kings maintained elements of pre-Islamic religious rites – practices that were still important to a large group of the population that had not embraced Islam in its totality (Crowder 1962: 81). The Habe kings attempted to straddle competing forms of beliefs as a way of upholding their rule over their states. It is here that an issue arose, as many Islamic scholars at the time viewed such practices as violating Islam. Tensions were to come to a head in the Hausa kingdom of Gobir, which by the 18th century had started to emerge as a hegemonic force in the region.

Gobir developed military tactics that allowed it to gain supremacy. Its armies were able to mount long sieges on towns and settlements, leading to the sacking of cities and towns in several states of Hausaland. By the 1750s, Gobir's actions against the kingdom of Zamfara climaxed in the devastation of the latter and the break-up of its government (Falola et al. 2007: 4). As a result of Gobir's newfound prominence, the state was able to agitate and maintain further hostile relationships with other states in the region, namely, Kwani, Zabarma, and Katsina. At the same time, however, the rulers of Gobir, and indeed many of the Hausa states, were accumulating vast amounts of wealth and behaving in ways that veered away from Islamically orthodox standards of morality.

In Gobir, as well as other Hausa states, there was an increased pressure for reform towards the theocratic model, to (re)establishing Islam as the governing ideology, and to ensuring that people – rulers and subjects alike – would live in accordance with *shari'a*. Such calls for reform came from members of the scholarly community who were less involved in the administration and more protective of the pure form of *shari'a*. In essence these were "free" scholars – they did not rely on the patronage of rulers to maintain their positions or salaries and so were able to speak at liberty to critique and to call for change. At times, the 'tension between scholars and administrators erupted into open conflict,' and there was a belief that in such circumstances a 'self-proclaimed renewer, a *mujaddid*, would come forward to lead the forces of reform' (Brenner 1979: 160).

It was not uncommon for such reforming scholars to declare that rulers had abandoned their religious obligations and as such should be regarded as apostates: 'jihad might be proclaimed calling upon true members of the faith to join in a struggle to establish, or re-establish, the proper religious foundations of government' (Brenner 1979: 160). This is a form of *takfir*, a controversial concept in Islam that allows for a believer to excommunicate another (nominal) believer, thus making them a legitimate target of attack. Such tactics are still used today by movements such as Boko Haram and the so-called Islamic State of Iraq and Syria, amongst others. At the court of Gobir, Usman dan Fodio had been among the most respected of scholars and, at the same time, a vocal critic of non-Islamic practices. It was he who would later go on to drive the movement for jihad and the restructuring of the socio-political order.

The Fulani factor: ties that bind

In the Nigerian context, Usman dan Fodio was the most famous and successful of the reforming scholars. The impact of his teachings and subsequent jihad in Hausaland were transformative, and the Sokoto Caliphate he established endured into the British colonization of the region and still carries resonance to this day. Dan Fodio was born in Gobir State in 1754. He received a Qur'anic education from his father and then studied with the firebrand Touareg scholar Sheikh Jibril Umar (discussed below). Hagiographical accounts of dan Fodio speak of his grasp of learning from a young age, of his piety and regard for Islamic mysticism. He settled at Degel in Gobir in the 1790s, and from there his fame continued to spread and attract students and scholars. He demanded complete acceptance of the spiritual and moral values of Islam and condemned corrupt and unjust governments which, against the teachings of the Qur'an, oppressed the poor and the weak (Webster & Bohen 1970: 6).

Dan Fodio was a Fulani, a large group of peoples who had settled peacefully in Hausaland more than 400 hundred years earlier. By the end of the 16th century they were established throughout the western Sudan from Senegal to the Cameroons. The majority of the Fulani were nomadic cattle owners devoted to an animistic religion, but a number had settled in towns, often intermarrying with the local population (Crowder 1962: 80). It was the town Fulani that became the propagators of Islam, not just in Nigeria, but across Sudanic Africa. In Hausaland, the Fulani, valued for their learning, gained high positions in the royal courts of the Hausa kings, and by 'the turn of the 18th century their increasing political and economic influence in the northern states gave the local rulers considerable concern for disquiet, especially since they formed a class at the vanguard of movements for religious and intellectual reform' (Crowder 1962: 80).

Tied to the Fulani's deep religiosity at the time were notions of the Fulani as a distinct group of people, a people elevated for the purpose of ushering in God's kingdom. This is captured in Fulani origin myths (Johnston 1967):

> One version describes the marriage of a Moslem Arab . . . identified as Ukuba, to a woman of the Sudan called Bajjo Mangu. One day the mother goes to the well and leaves her youngest child in the care of its brothers. On her return she overhears the brother comforting the child in a strange language. She tells her husband, who predicts that this is a sign that the child will be the founder of a new people who will not speak Arabic, but will nevertheless be the saviors of Islam.

The importance of this legend is that Islam emerges as a key feature in Fulani identity. From the Fulani perspective, they were a people of whom great things were prophesied – they were heralded as the saviors of Islam. This notion resounded through the Fulani-led jihads of Islamic revivalism in the 19th century. The fact that the Fulani saw themselves as having descended from Arab lineage may have helped to set them apart from the wider black African populations that they came to live amongst, as well as endowing a sense of religious superiority.

Even though the Fulani were later converts to Islam than both the Hausa and Kanuri peoples, it seems that they were better Islamized, with Islam being a defining component of their identity. Fulani were among the most prominent religious scholars in the courts of the Hausa chiefs. One account has it that the Fulani religious scholars 'preached the *shari'a*, taught in the palaces of the Hausa rulers, strove to rationalize the actions of the rulers and to moralize their conduct . . . their leadership qualities, sense of purpose, and religious fervor contrasted strongly with the nature of the Hausa' (Nur-Awaleh 2006). Major Dixon Denham, Dr. Oudney, and Commander Hugh Clapperton, European explorers to Hausaland and Borno from 1823–1825, state that the 'Fulani as Moslems, moreover, were generally much stricter than the more genial and worldly Hausas and Kanuri' (Johnston & Muffet 1973: 65). The increase in religiosity and adherence to the tenets of Islam, as encouraged by the Fulani throughout Hausaland, helped to alter the balance of power towards Fulani ideals of governance (Trimingham 1959):

> Islam introduced an anarchic element [in Hausa society], that the law of God was absolute. Friction was therefore eminent between the ruling Hausa aristocracy and the ecclesiastic body composed mainly of the

Fulani, who claimed to know the divine will of Allah. Fulani ulama and scholars had to stress religion as the new binding force and solicited the cooperation of the ruling Hausa elites to defend the faith.

Injustices against the Fulani were seen as 'injustices not only against their ethnic group but also against the religion of Islam' (Adeleye 1971). Prior to the 19th century jihad, which ushered in the Sokoto Caliphate, the Fulani were largely outside the pale of government, and with Islam playing so prominent a role in their identity, the 'Fulani were more favorably placed to identify abuses against Islamic tenets than their counterpart indigenous Muslims, many of whom had vested interests in the existing system' (Adeleye 1971). It is therefore not strange that religious reform should have found its staunchest votaries among the Fulani. The discontent of the Fulani reformers arose not just from concerns over deviations in correct Islamic practice – such as Muslim men marrying more than four wives, failing to pray correctly, or not inheriting according to the *shari'a* – but from the fact that the society in which they lived was governed in a manner and through institutions that were not those of Islam. This charge returned as a central aspect of Boko Haram sermons and was a rallying point for the movement's push towards carving out Islamic territory in the region. This is clear in a speech by Saniu Umar (2009), an interim leader of Boko Haram, who, directly after the killing of Mohammad Yusuf, said:

> In this case, our emphasis is on western styles of life which includes constitutional provision as it relates to, the rights and privileges of women, the idea of homosexuality, lesbianism, sanctions in the cases of terrible crimes like drug trafficking, rape of infants, multi-party democracy in majority Muslim countries like Nigeria, blue films, prostitution, drinking beer and alcohol and many others that are opposed to Islamic civilization.[5]

As with Fulani scholars who frequently pointed to the immoral and impure actions of the Hausa as violations of Islam, so too do Boko Haram with today's leaders of Nigeria.

Dan Fodio's jihad

Much like other reformers of his time, and those to follow in later years, Dan Fodio's main charge against governance in his locality was that Islam was being ignored and that society had fallen into degeneracy. He wrote that the rulers had gone astray from the path of Allah and raised the flag of worldliness above the flag of Islam and were thus *kufar* – or unbelievers

(Adeleye 1971). His purpose, he reiterated, was to 'revive the Sunna and annihilate satanic innovations that had crept into the social fabric,' in short, to establish a society that approximated as closely as possible the original prophetic community (Ibraheem 2009: 115). From circa 1798, when he was 36 years old, until the outbreak of the jihad in 1804, it is claimed that dan Fodio experienced visions in which he came face-to-face with the prophet Mohammad and with Abd al-Qadir al-Jilani, the 12th-century founder of the Sufi Qadiriyya order. He believed that al-Jilani appointed him as his representative in the Sudan and handed to him the 'Sword of Truth' to use against the enemies of God (Hiskett 1984: 160). It is through such visions that he came to believe that he had been vested with the mantle to actively combat the decaying form of Islam around him and strive for the creation of a new society in which the *shari'a* would be supreme. While the narrative gives a compelling allure to dan Fodio and his achievements, this aspect of dan Fodio's life has been challenged, as the 'fragments of the text on which it is based could be later forgeries, made at a time when people wanted to reassert the Shehu's Sufi roots' (Walker 2016: 16).

Dan Fodio held the rulers responsible for un-Islamic practices, and, ultimately, it was the actions of the new ruler of Gobir that ignited jihad. Dan Fodio lamented

> earning a living from talismans, obtaining the post of a *qadi* [judge] through bribery, accepting favors after appointment, misappropriating the zakat, and the complete neglect of Qur'anic studies. He further bemoaned the immodest behavior of women, lack of education for women, gambling, fraudulent practices in the market, clowning, cheating, pimping etc.
>
> (Nur-Awaleh 2006)

In the course of his preaching dan Fodio became increasingly involved in the politics of the Gobir court, especially as a means of attempting to reform the chief of Gobir and his successor. Dan Fodio demanded the king of Gobir: '1. To allow me to call people to God in your country; 2. Not to stop anybody who intends to respond to my call; 3. To treat with respect any man with a turban; 4. To free all political prisoners; and 5. Not to burden the subjects with taxes' (Falola et al. 2007: 8). While the old chief of Gobir gave way to some of dan Fodio's demands, the new ruler, fearing the increased power of the reformist Muslim community, decreed that '1. No man should become a Muslim unless a Muslim-born; 2. All converts should revert to their original faith; 3. Men should no longer wear a turban; and women should no longer veil themselves; 4. Nobody except Usman dan Fodio himself should preach Islam' (Falola et al. 2007: 8).

Dan Fodio, viewing the hostility of the governing elites, an attempt on his own life, and an incompatibility with being able to live life according to the principles of Islam, issued a fatwa on *hijra* – or emigrating from the land of unbelievers to a place where they could practice their religion in freedom. This move was to mirror what the prophet Mohammad did in 622 AD after being warned of a plot to assassinate him. Mohammad escaped out of Mecca with Abu Bakr and fled for Medina. The act of *hijra* from what is perceived as a land of unbelief to a place in which there is freedom to practice Islam may also be seen as a search for justice, honor, safety, and the rule of law. Yet, such a move 'is only a temporary expedient and Muslims are expected to prepare themselves during the period of respite for the ulti-mate confrontation with unbelievers, with the sole aim of establishing a *dar al-Islam* [abode of Islam] in the area from which they have fled' (Suliman 2009: 186). There are remarkable similarities between Dan Fodio's *hijra* and subsequent armed jihad to the actions taken by Boko Haram's own *hijra* from Maiduguri to rural northern Yobe State in 2003 and its ensuing violent actions several years later (Pieri & Zenn 2016: 75). Boko Haram's leaders, who admire dan Fodio, saw a clear example in the historical record of how to proceed in their own attempts to establish Islamic territory and acted upon that lesson. It is clear that Dan Fodio's actions still have an impor-tant significance for Boko Haram leaders and their followers in modern-day Nigeria.

Dan Fodio's *hijra* was in effect a threat, in that it highlighted to his own people and to the Sultan of Gobir that preparations would take place for jihad just as it had in the time of Mohammad: this meant 'emigration from the land of unbelievers, election of a leader, and by implication, war. Since the Shaikh's community was virtually self-governing, the call to emigrate was an invitation to join the community' (Last & Al-Hajj 1965: 236). Once the decision for *hijra* was taken, it forced the Sultan of Gobir to take action, for a large number of dan Fodio's followers throughout the region started to join the community in exile. When the armies of the state of Gobir attacked the Muslims, their position as unbelievers was defined: 'all those who fought the Muslims were either unbelievers or apostates. The term "Muslims" is consistently used for the followers of the Sheikh in Sokoto, and there is no reason to think that they did not regard their enemies as non-Muslims' (Last & Al-Hajj 1965: 236).

Dan Fodio's victory in Gobir set off the Fulani campaign in other Hausa kingdoms. Even the Fulani living in the ancient kingdom of Borno rose in revolt against the Mai there. The outlying campaigns, although inspired by dan Fodio, were conducted by Fulani clan leaders in these kingdoms. The clan leaders were recognized by dan Fodio as his 'flag-bearers,' and when they were successful, they became emirs of the territories they had conquered (Hiskett 1984: 165). These they held as largely independent prin-cipalities, but in allegiance to dan Fodio. Many Fulani pastoralists and some Hausa peasants and merchants shared dan Fodio's sentiments and joined his forces. Many others were forced to ally themselves with the jihad for fear of attack by the Fulani. The Fulani were rallied in each of the capitals of the Hausa states, and their religious zeal enabled them to amass numerous victories (VerEecke 1985: 165). By 1809, all Hausa city-states had been conquered, although incursions into the heart of Borno had been unsuccess-ful. The leaders of the Sokoto jihad claimed that the spread of the jihad into the territories of the Muslim Empire of Borno was reasonable because the Mai had allowed pagan practices under his rule and that the Fulani had been persecuted in favor of the pagan Hausa dynasties (Webster & Bohen 1970: 35). The charges against Borno were 'that Borno was polytheistic and a land of unbelief . . . that Borno was aiding the Hausa kings and therefore aligned with the unbelievers, and that Borno attacked them [the Fulani] and they were fighting in self-defense' (Last & Al-Hajj 1965: 238).

Consequences of the jihad

Dan Fodio's jihad had multiple consequences, the most obvious being the transformation of the governing structures of the territories that came under the rule of the caliphate. His caliphate was the largest political unit in 19th-century west Africa, made up of 15 major emirates spread over 180,000 square miles, which required four months to cross from east to west and about two months from north to south (Webster & Bohen 1970: 14). The former Hausa kingdoms, now ruled by Fulani emirs, together with the newly acquired pagan provinces were held together by common allegiance to the Commander of the Faithful at one and the same time a spiritual and tem-poral ruler. Each province paid tribute to Sokoto, and all matters of higher administration were referred to the capital (Crowder 1962: 93).

The jihad served to change Islam from a religion of scholars and elites into the official state ideology of a new empire. While it took a number of generations for the population as a whole to become more orthodox in their practice of Islam, the consequences for women in particular were much more immediate and profound. Norms for acceptable behavior by Muslim women were forcefully introduced, stressing their proper place as the home: 'Here they were expected to remain secluded, carry out domestic labor and childcare responsibilities, engaging in income earning activities, praying alone, and participating in a social life involving them in relations with other females, children and kin' (Coles & Mack 1991: 6).

While dan Fodio's jihad was not able to conquer the Borno empire, it did have a number of consequences for its two neighbors. By 1808,

Borno was weak, fractured, and fearful that it would succumb to dan Fodio's forces. The ruling Sultan of Borno, Mai Muhammadu Lefiami, was forced to call upon the assistance of Sheikh Muhammad el-Amin el-Kanemi (Johnston & Muffett 1973: 66). El-Kanemi carried influence with his fellow Kanembu, who were renowned as pikemen, and he promoted the Sultan's cause among the Shuwa Arabs living in Borno. By bringing in these reinforcements and rallying the demoralized Kanuri, he turned the tide of the war. After inconclusive fighting between armies loyal to Borno and to Sokoto, both sides realized that the sandy plains of central Borno were not worth their price in blood. The Fulani therefore consolidated their gains in the west while the Kanuri fell back on Lake Chad in the east (Johnston & Muffett 1973: 66). The Kanemi family, who would go on to take control over the Borno territories and oust the traditional ruling Mais, became a central voice in the negotiations between Borno and Sokoto. Kanemi challenged the legitimacy of dan Fodio's attacks against Borno – a dispute that deeply disturbed the Sokoto leaders intent on building an Islamic state and on scrupulously observing *shari'a* law. Al-Kanemi's argument throughout the dispute was simple and consistent (Last & Al-Hajj 1965: 239):

> The people of Borno, while admittedly being superstitious, were not polytheists at heart; they were fighting to defend themselves and their property. To the charge that they helped the Hausa he makes no answer; what ever help it was (and it cannot have been great), it was not given in his time. He therefore asks the Shaikh to call off the Fulani attacks, but at the same time never refers disparagingly to the Shaikh himself or to his work. The Shaikh argued that he could not stop the Fulani because that would be illegal, seeing that the people of Borno were unbelievers since they had helped the Hausa.

In this sense it is clear that Boko Haram better align themselves with the view put forward by dan Fodio, rather than with Kanemi's more moderate argument. Even though Boko Haram have a predominantly Kanuri base, and the movement's strongholds are within the boundaries of the former Kanem-Borno Empire, it is clear that ideologically they align with dan Fodio. For Boko Haram leaders, ethnicity may remain an important consideration in terms of recruitment strategy, but at the forefront belief is placed before ethnicity. The focus is on implementing a Salafi Islam and to take what dan Fodio did in northwestern Nigeria and to spread this to northeastern Nigeria. The goal is to create an Islamic territory in which Islamic governance may be implemented in purity and totality.

The arrival of the British

The situation between Borno and Sokoto would stabilize, and the geo-political map in northern Nigeria would not change much until the advent of British colonialism in the region which began in July 1886 with the activities of the Royal Niger Company (a chartered company which had been granted administrative influence over in its areas of operation on behalf of the British government). The main objective of the company was to secure the cooperation of traditional rulers in ensuring peaceful conditions for trade that were advantageous to British interests. While this policy was successful for a decade, after 1895 colonial policy in west Africa was starting to change, mainly in response to the European "scramble for Africa." Thereafter, policies were directed towards the acquisition of land as opposed to spheres of influence, with the formal takeover of Nigeria coming in 1900. The Company's southern territories in the Niger Delta were amalgamated into the Niger Coast protectorate and came to be known as the Protectorate of Southern Nigeria. The Company's northern territories became the Protectorate of Northern Nigeria, with Fredrick Lugard, one of the chief architects of Britain's policy of indirect rule, appointed as the first High Commissioner of the North. The two territories were later to be amalgamated, and achieved independence as a unified Nigeria.

The formal British takeover of these territories had a transformative effect on the governance and administration of the region. Most notable was the complete disregard for ethnic, religious, and cultural divides that existed in the country and the imposition of a single (and artificial) Nigerian identity on all. It is true that the British outlawed slavery, introduced western education in the south, and accommodated local customs that did not contradict what the British called the 'laws of humanity' (Lugard 1904), but the carving up of the Borno empire, amalgamating a part of it with Sokoto and then merging the two with a non-Muslim south, became unforgivable in the eyes of many. Indeed, the repudiation of the Nigerian state, which is seen as a product of British colonialism, remains a central goal of Boko Haram today.

The impact of Wahhabism

Dan Fodio's jihad in Hausaland was just one of a series of movements in west Africa and beyond that called for and enacted major change at the time. Many movements were inspired in one way or another by the Wahhabis of Arabia in the 18th century and can be seen as part of a process of pre-modern "globalization" among Muslim states, spurred on through the intermingling of people during the Hajj pilgrimage. As a result of the renewed zeal for a return to what was regarded as correct Islamic practice based on the examples of Mohammad and his companions, the number of pilgrims to Arabia from Hausaland and Borno continued to increase. The Hijaz was seen as the cradle of Islam and the spiritual home of all Muslims, with the annual congregation at Mecca and Medina instilling in those Muslims who travelled there a sense of pride and the greatness of Islam (Alkali 1985: 134). At the same time, it had the effect of bringing people from all over the Muslim world into contact with the then emerging movement of Wahhabism – a movement that would go on to form the founding ideology of the Kingdom of Saudi Arabia. Pilgrims would perceive Wahhabi Islam as more authentic, especially because of its proximity to the holy places, and then export elements of the ideology back to their home regions. One such person was dan Fodio's teacher, Malam Jibril.

Dan Fodio's theology, however, as well as that of his adherents, was rooted in Maliki orthodoxy, and the overwhelming majority of religious scholars they quoted belonged to this school. Moreover, dan Fodio was initiated into the Qadiriyya – a Sufi brotherhood that he was active in – to the point of apparently experiencing visions (Hiskett 1984: 160). Dan Fodio wrote spiritual poetry, composed songs, and engaged in many traditional Sufi activities, many of which were anathema to the strictly purist Wahhabis. Nevertheless, dan Fodio's doctrines had a strong element not only of reform but of radical and fundamental reform. The question therefore remains as to whether there were any links between those who sought to initiate jihad in west Africa and other Islamic reformers of the day, particularly the Wahhabis with whom at first sight they seemed to have much in common.

In the works of Mallam Abullahi, dan Fodio's brother, there are references to Ibn Hanbali, whose writings influenced Al-Wahhab, perhaps showing that the Fulani reformers were acquainted with the sources on which Wahhabism drew (Johnston 1967: 103). Yet, there are many Islamic movements and Muslims that draw on Hanbali theology and who do not turn towards violent extremism. Furthermore, there have been reformist strands in all four schools of Islam that have had Salafist undertones. Yet it is difficult to deny the impact of Wahhabism on the milieu of the time. One of the most important was through returning pilgrims from Arabia, who had come into contact with the then emerging Wahhabi ideology. Among those who had made the pilgrimage were two men who exerted influence on dan Fodio, namely his tutor, Mallam Jibril, and his paternal uncle, Muhammad dan Raji, in 1794 (Johnston 1967: 103). As Hiskett (1973) notes, Jibril was an intense and zealous Muslim iconoclast who held the most rigorous views concerning the status of sinners. He taught that disobedience to *shari'a* law was a sin sufficient to invalidate a man's Islamic belief and turn him into an unbeliever destined for eternal punishment in the fires of hell. His views are 'likely to have evolved as a result of his long exposure to the teachings of the Wahhabis . . . in Arabia, during the years Jibril spent studying there.' Jibril was one of dan Fodio's most important teachers and one of the leading scholars around Gobir. He was strict; in effect he argued that to commit major sins constituted unbelief. The sins he classed as constituting unbelief were (Last & Al-Hajj 1965: 233):

> i) not keeping the *shari'a* law, ii) nakedness in the presence of women, iii) mixing with women in public, iv) depriving the orphan of his property, v) having more than four wives, vi) inheriting the widows of one's relations, vii) following the pre-Islamic practices of one's ancestors. Those who do these things are doing what no believer should do and are therefore regarded as unbelievers.

Jibril's influence on dan Fodio was as much provocative as informative because, despite his great veneration for his teacher, dan Fodio (at least early on) rejected his extreme religious radicalism. However, the intransigence that he met with, and the fierceness with which his opponents reacted in defense of their own points of view, gradually hardened his attitudes. Even though he may not have desired war as a means of achieving his ends, he came increasingly to accept the necessity for it. Later in life, depressed by the disappointments that afflicted him after the jihad, the iron of Jibril's teaching entered more deeply into his soul. He then became stern and uncompromising, both to his enemies and to those of his own community who fell short of his own high ideals (Las & Al-Hajj 1965: 233).

There were marked resemblances between the fundamentalism of the Wahhabis and that of the Fulani, and between the two brands of "puritanism" which flowed from these doctrines. For example, one point which Dan Fodio emphasized in his writings was the importance of studying the lives of the early caliphs and his personal predilection for a system of government as starkly simple as theirs. Similarly, many of the reforms which he advocated were identical to those that the Wahhabis had already introduced – both focused on the politics of purity and the enforcement of high moral codes as restorative for the health of society. Though Dan Fodio may have been influenced by Wahhabism, it is not accurate to label the Fulani reformation as part of the Wahhabi movement, and there were important differences. Dan Fodio looked back to the early days of the Caliphal period as offering the ideal system of Islamic government but relied much more on the jurists of the Abbasid Caliphate than on the earlier authorities, while the administrative machine governing his caliphate was nothing like the simple society of Medina, but a complex hierarchy akin to that of the Abbasids (Johnston 1967: 103). Yet, most important was that the Wahhabis' denial of the authority of the four Orthodox jurists of Islam found no place in the beliefs of the Fulani. On balance, therefore, while the reforming movement in Hausaland was influenced by Wahhabism, it was certainly not inspired by the Wahhabis, and it was always separated from them by principal differences of dogma and practice (Johnston 1967: 103). Instead, dan Fodio's movement was part of the wider trend of Islamic revivalism that was occurring in Sudanic and west Africa at the turn of the 19th century. Significant is that Sufism can be as much a vehicle for radical and violent reform as Salafi strands of Islam. This contested nature of dan Fodio is not recognized by Boko Haram, whose leaders' instead stress his Salafi lineage and draw a direct line between Ibn Wahhab, dan Fodio, and Salafi jihadists such as Abubakr al-Baghdadi.

Understanding the past, shaping the future

Boko Haram leaders articulated the goal of establishing an Islamic state in northern Nigeria as early as 2002, almost a decade before Abubakar Shekau declared jihad in July 2010. This notion of carving out an Islamic territory is not a new concept thought up by Boko Haram but rather a part of Nigeria's historical and religious context, especially in Usman dan Fodio's jihad which mobilized to fight against the existing "infidel" (predominantly Hausa) Muslim power structures of the region in order to implement his vision of an Islamic state. Dan Fodio ultimately succeeded in toppling the Hausa Muslim states of northern Nigeria and in their place established the Sokoto Caliphate. This Caliphate existed for 100 years until the British imposed colonial rule over northern Nigeria. The present-day sultans and emirs in the areas of the former Sokoto Caliphate, who are the descendants of dan Fodio and his emirs, have maintained their status as traditional religious rulers but, in most cases, no longer have any formal political or military authority.

The concept of a caliphate *with* political and military authority has, however, continued to resonate with Nigerian Islamists in contemporary times. This desire for a new caliphate was harnessed and promoted by Boko Haram, whose ideology, militant successes, and declaration of an Islamic state in 2014 are perhaps the closest Nigerian Muslims have come to reviving an Islamic state since the end of the Sokoto Caliphate. Boko Haram leaders are inspired and motivated by dan Fodio's jihad. Their sermons, publications, and statements make it clear that their aim is to (re)create that caliphate with "Boko Haram-approved" leaders replacing the current "infidel" Muslim traditional leaders, who are regarded as guilty of mixing Islam with western notions of democracy, secularism, and education (Pieri & Zenn 2017: 58). However, this chapter shows that unlike dan Fodio, whose jihad emanated from the Fulani lands in Northwestern Nigeria, Boko Haram's jihad is from the traditional Kanuri homelands.

It is in this context that Boko Haram sees itself as a present-day manifestation of dan Fodio's jihad, using the same core arguments as dan Fodio to attack rival Islamic leaders – albeit in the heartlands of Kanuri territories. Shekau realigned Boko Haram with the most visible jihadist trends of this era – Abubakar al-Baghdadi's Islamic State – which has seemingly led to more emboldened Boko Haram attacks, including occupying and holding territory, and new rhetoric about the caliphate in Nigeria consonant with al-Baghdadi's so-called caliphate in Iraq and Syria. Boko Haram is not an aberration in Nigerian history or in present-day global circumstances. The tendency to write off the movement as a one-hit wonder that will easily be dismissed in the annals of Nigerian history is likely incorrect. Rather, Boko Haram has the necessary ethno-historical and religious underpinning to become a long-lasting movement whose impact on Nigerian and African security can only be rolled back and countered once the strength of the bases for its existence are recognized and appropriate strategies to meet the reality of the threats developed.

Notes

1 Yusuf, M. 2008. 'History of the Muslims', in Kassim, A. and Nwankpa, M. (eds.). *The Boko Haram Reader: From Nigerian Preachers to the Islamic State*. Oxford and New York: Oxford University Press, pp. 85–102.
2 Mai was the traditional title of the Muslim rulers of the Kanem-Borno Empire.
3 Yusuf, M. 2008. 'History of the Muslims', in Kassim, A. and Nwankpa, M. (eds.). *The Boko Haram Reader: From Nigerian Preachers to the Islamic State*. Oxford and New York: Oxford University Press.
4 Also in this strand of revivalist Islam may be added the thought of Shah Walliullah of Delhi, India (Pieri 2015).
5 Umar, S. 2009. 'Statement of Sani Umaru', in Kassim, A. and Nwankpa, M. (eds.). *The Boko Haram Reader: From Nigerian Preachers to the Islamic State*. Oxford: Oxford University Press, pp. 207–208.

3   The prelude to violence

Introduction

This chapter investigates corruption as a driving factor in Boko Haram's formation, mobilization, and ultimate shift to violence. Since turning to violence in 2009, Boko Haram became a threat to Nigeria and the neighboring Lake Chad Basin (LCB). Between 2009 and 2017, over 20,000 people were killed and more than 2 million displaced (BBC 2018). In 2017 alone, the movement was responsible for killing over 900 people, a small increase on 2016 (BBC 2018). Though the costs of violence are tragic, another facet of Boko Haram's potency lies in its ability to symbolize weaknesses in the Nigerian state. Despite repeated claims from President Buhari since 2016 that Boko Haram has been defeated (Utietiang 2016; Toromade 2018), the movement continues to not only exist but also to carry out widely publicized attacks and kidnappings (for example the kidnapping in January 2018 of 110 schoolgirls in the town of Dapchi) and, as such, belies the idea that the Nigerian state has a monopoly on the legitimate use of violence in the country.

The argument in this chapter is that the high level of corruption evidenced in the Nigerian state has been key in contributing to the success of Boko Haram, particularly in its formative period. The fragility of the Nigerian state's legitimacy opened space for new aspirants to power and it is in this context that Boko Haram may be understood as one of those contenders, though distinguished in part by its willingness to engage in violence. Boko Haram's evolution from a social movement into a *takfiri* jihadist group, however, has done much to erode that initial support. Since 2009, under the leadership of Abubakar Shekau, Boko Haram uses the framework of Salafi-jihadism to violently act for political change in the region, though the push factors for support of the movement have little to do with religion per se (Deckard et al. 2015). To Boko Haram, the Nigerian state is an illegitimate colonial construct, defined by corruption and a rejection of an Islamic order, and so needs to be destroyed.

Part of Mohammad Yusuf's success was to take genuine social and economic grievances, especially mounting anger over government corruption, and to package the solution within an Islamic framework that called for his followers to migrate away from the jurisdiction of the Nigerian state and put in its place the reestablishment of pre-colonial forms of governance, namely an Islamic state. While corruption was an important driver in Boko Haram's formative period, it should not be overstated as the only factor, nor indeed as a factor that can be separated from Yusuf's broader worldview and ideology. Yusuf's objective was not solely to combat corruption but rather to usher in an Islamic form of governance as the antidote to corruption and social ills. It should be remembered that Yusuf's 'ideal of social justice also had to be according to the precepts of *shari'a* and cannot be interpreted as a fight against corruption in the same fashion as *Transparency International*' (Perouse de Montclos 2017: 29).

The chapter begins through contextualizing the issue of corruption within Nigeria, arguing that decades of plundering of the nation's wealth, economic mismanagement, and failure to integrate Nigeria in to a cohesive whole created a situation in which movements such as Boko Haram were able to emerge. The section is based on survey data collected in 2013, thereby providing a snapshot on perceptions of corruption at the time when Boko Haram was turning violent. Corruption served an important function in acting as a clear grievance and as a means to highlight the inadequacies of the Nigerian state. The chapter will continue with outlining the foundation of Boko Haram, how Yusuf and other leaders were able to seize on the issue of corruption to challenge the Nigerian state in a way that chimed with local populations in the northeast of the country. The chapter also provides an organizational structure of Boko Haram before drawing on a discourse analysis of its leaders' speeches to chart how Boko Haram turned from a movement focused on righting wrongs in society, albeit from an Islamist perspective, to one based on violent jihad.

The role of corruption in Nigeria

On my first trip to Nigeria, in late 2013, the one thing that stood out to me more than anything else was the level of corruption that seemed to be ingrained into almost every aspect of society. Though I had heard that Nigeria was corrupt, I was not prepared for the level of corruption that I would face on a daily basis. This included sometimes having to pay small amounts of money to access research materials in a library where those materials were meant to be freely accessible and having to pay money to police officers to be allowed through checkpoints on the road. Many of the participants in my research recounted stories of what they called the "corruption economy" in Nigeria, which draws in almost every citizen. All of my participants (from senior Islamic scholars to Internally Displaced Persons (IDPs)) stated that corruption is the most pressing issue facing Nigeria, even more so than Boko Haram itself. Indeed, corruption is unavoidable in any discussion of Nigeria, a fact not lost on President Buhari (2016), who talked of corruption as a 'hydra-headed monster and a cankerworm that undermines' the fabric of society.

According to Transparency International's (2018) Corruption Index for 2017, an index which ranks 180 countries and territories by their perceived levels of public-sector corruption according to experts and businesspeople, Nigeria was placed at 148 out of 180, scoring just 27 out of 100 points. Despite numerous pledges to tackle corruption in Nigeria by successive governments, the score has remained consistent for the past decade. Nigeria is also more corrupt when compared to other countries that have similar levels of wealth, irrespective of location, and Nigeria further bucks the trend of decreasing corruption when levels of national wealth increase. It is important to note, however, that even though corruption is rampant irrespective of region, the state, especially at the subnational level, has been able to perform many of its duties, including the delivery of public services (Deckard & Pieri 2017: 373). Issues have arisen because different parts of the state at the subnational level have been more effective than others. The north, and particularly the northeast, of the country has fallen behind in access to education and health care, and anti-state grievances in these regions of the country are more pronounced (Pieri & Barkindo 2016: 137–138). This, added to other pre-existing factors such as historical grievance, a rise of more extremist forms of Islam, and issues over ethno-territorial legitimacy, has created an atmosphere in which some Nigerians contemplated supporting violent non-state actors such as Boko Haram, especially in its early phases.

Corruption has further affected Nigeria's military capabilities and capacity. Soldiers deployed to fight Boko Haram in northeastern Nigeria have claimed that their budgeted allowance for dangerous field duties is siphoned off by commanders more interested in lining their own pockets (Hassan & Pieri 2018). Ammunition and arms are budgeted and paid for, but not all supplies reach the front lines, 'either because they are diverted to the black market, or because the money actually went into a procurer's pocket' (Baker 2015). Soldiers have described how they are sent out to fight Boko Haram with rocket-propelled grenades while having only a dozen bullets each. The soldiers complained that they 'had to cover medical expenses for wounds received in battle, and that the spouses of dead soldiers were only granted a minimal stipend' (Baker 2015).

The issue of corruption in Nigeria has permeated every function of governance, including the ways in which the state provides day-to-day security to the population. Extrajudicial killings at the hands of the police force in Nigeria have become frequent and serve to weaken the state's legitimacy. In 2016 alone, Nigerian police were accused of extrajudicially killing over 40 citizens and at the same time collecting increasing amounts of bribe payments (Ajayi 2017). While historically in Nigeria extrajudicial killings occurred outside the state's purview, for example by lynch mobs (Elechi 2003), such killings have become increasingly incorporated into the tactics of the police and military, thus denying trial by courts (Ojo 2010). Perhaps the most prominent extrajudicial killing was that of Boko Haram's leader, Mohammad Yusuf (see ahead), which is considered to have been a significant push factor in the movement's radicalization.

Over the past several years, the focus of my research has been on the drivers of Boko Haram violence, and due to this, I was privileged to work as part of a larger team at the University of South Florida that looked at data on the perceptions of corruption in Nigeria and the extent to which corruption is correlated with support for and beliefs about Boko Haram (Deckard & Pieri 2017; Deckard et al. 2015). Our research at the time hypothesized that perceptions of high levels of corruption would correlate with relatively greater levels of support for Boko Haram and a more positive belief set regarding the organization as respondents demonstrated decreased confidence in the Nigerian government (Decakard & Pieri 2018: 377). To investigate this we utilized the results of a survey completed by Gallup in Nigeria in 2013. Though much has changed since 2013, not least the increased ruthlessness of Boko Haram, and as such making the results less applicable to today's context, the data does provide a snapshot of attitudes at the point when Boko Haram transformed into a violent organization and is thus important in helping us to understand how the movement evolved over time.

The face-to-face surveys included both open- and close-ended questions and were completed by 10,482 Nigerian residents from across every region of the country. The survey covered a range of topics, including religion, family, politics, household amenities, and demographic characteristics, and established the extent to which respondents supported violence generally and their views of Boko Haram specifically. We found corruption to be a significant predictor of support for Boko Haram. The likelihood of perceiving Boko Haram as a positive influence on Nigeria was significantly correlated with the perception that corruption is Nigeria's biggest problem. Respondents who identified corruption as Nigeria's largest problem were almost twice as likely (181%) to see Boko Haram as a positive influence than those who saw corruption as less important (Deckard & Pieri 2018: 381). We further found that male respondents, respondents from wealthier households, and those who identified as unemployed had elevated likelihoods of believing Boko Haram to be a positive influence. At the other end of the spectrum, those who thought the Nigerian government to be ineffective against fighting terrorism, who are older, or who are more religious had decreased odds of believing Boko Haram to be a positive influence (Deckard & Pieri 2017: 381).

Those who perceived Boko Haram as successful in 2013 were also highly correlated with the perception that corruption is the biggest problem in the nation. The belief that corruption is the largest problem in Nigeria was associated with odds of seeing Boko Haram as a positive influence that are 21% greater than those associated with a respondent who believed that other issues are more problematic (Deckard & Pieri 2017: 381). From our data, we were able to conclude that Muslim men who believed corruption to be Nigeria's largest problem also had the highest likelihood of believing Boko Haram to be a successful organization. It should be noted that even though a certain group of people viewed Boko Haram as a successful organization in 2013, it did not mean that those people flocked to join its ranks.

The finding that corruption is a fundamental factor in the support or sympathy for Boko Haram in Nigeria is telling, and it reveals a crisis in Nigerian society that precedes Boko Haram itself – namely, the widespread failure of democratic institutions in Nigeria and an attendant lack of state legitimacy. This is not to suggest that many state institutions do not try to fulfil their civic roles, but to recognize that corruption is indeed widespread. This corruption exacerbates a myriad of factors that lead to deepening perceptions of the illegitimacy of the Nigerian state. Rather than being driven exclusively by religion, religiosity, ethnicity, amenities – or lack thereof – a significant amount of support for Boko Haram is driven by disgust with corruption, and indeed with the lack of autonomy, within the Nigerian state.

There are those who argue that poverty is a pivotal factor in explaining Boko Haram (Agbiboa 2013; Mustapha 2014: 171; UNDP 2017: 59), but my research suggests that corruption is a far more important factor. Recommendations from UNDP (2017) stipulate that in order to stem the effectiveness of Boko Haram, more should be done in terms of developing the northeast of Nigeria, allowing for economic opportunities and the increase of wealth. While this would benefit the region, it would by itself not stifle Boko Haram. As Cook (2014: 5–6) postulates, the argument suffers, for it,

> does not answer the question of why exactly Boko Haram in its numerous videos and statements does not stress economic issues, nor does it explain why given similar impoverished circumstances throughout Nigeria such a violent group would appear only in the northeast and not any other place.

Moreover, the results from our survey showed that it was not poverty that indicated support for Boko Haram, but rather prosperity: 'in these data prosperity largely predicts support for violence. This surprise may be related to dashed higher expectations among the near-elite, rather than among the poor or destitute' (Deckard et al. 2015: 523).

Mohammad Yusuf and the genesis of Boko Haram

Boko Haram did not emerge in a vacuum, but rather was deeply rooted within the Islamist history of the LCB, stemming back at least (in a conceptual way) to the jihad of Usman dan Fodio in 1804. There were also more immediate factors that spurred the movement on, including what Boko Haram leaders saw as the failure of the state or religious elites to implement strict *shari'a* law in the country's north, along with state corruption, state brutality, and continuing levels of inequality in the north, as well as a feeling of political disenfranchisement among many living in the northeast. These are all factors that Mohammad Yusuf discussed in his sermons and which were tied up in his early ideology. Indeed, in order to understand the impetus for Boko Haram, one must first gain insight into Yusuf himself, a young and charismatic preacher who was instrumental in garnering its support, and for his Islamist vision for Nigeria. Details about Yusuf's background and early years are sparse, with some contradictory accounts.

It is generally agreed that Yusuf was born in 1970 in Yobe State to a Kanuri family and, according to Barkindo (2017), received an Islamic education from prominent scholars in Nigeria, Chad, and Niger before going on to experiment with different forms of Islamic activism. This account is reinforced in *Slicing The Tumor*, a book said to have been written by two of Yusuf's sons, and released by the Islamic State West Africa Province (ISWAP) faction of Boko Haram in 2018:

> The sheikh grew up in a religious environment in Maiduguri, and he mastered the Qur'an in the Qur'an school his father ran, and he studied the sciences of Arabic and the sciences of Qur'an, hadith and jurisprudence . . . in the states of Borno and Yobe in particular and the north of Nigeria . . . and he joined the night course classes in the al-Kanemi institute.
>
> (ISWAP 2018)

In the early 1990s, Yusuf is said to have joined Ibrahim El-Zakzaky's Shi'a Islamic Movement in Nigeria, and this is again corroborated by the ISWAP document, although it explains that Yusuf was duped into this movement, not knowing it was Shi'a, and that upon finding out immediately re-oriented to more orthodox activities (ISWAP 2018).

Yusuf realigned himself with Sheikh Ja'afar Mahmood Adam of Kano, and the Izala movement (Barkindo 2017). Izala was inspired by a Wahhabist form of Islam which took shape under the tutelage of Sheikh Mahmud Abubakar Gumi (1922–1992) in 1978, and 'was a major impetus in the radicalization of Muslims in northern Nigeria' (Muhammad 2014: 22). Although not anti-establishment, Izala became 'critical of traditional rulers, of corruption in government, and of declining moral values of the society, without calling for a wholesale overthrow of the system.' (Muhammad 2014: 22) Ja'afar, believing that Izala did not go far enough, broke away and formed his own Salafist movement called *Ahl Al-Sunna*, in which Mohammad Yusuf was appointed leader of its youth wing.

There are also accounts of Yusuf involving himself with the so-called 'Nigerian Taliban' and its leader Muhammed Ali, a Nigerian graduate of the Islamic University in Khartoum, Sudan, who is said to have met with Osama bin Laden when the latter was leader of the proto-al-Qaeda organization based in Khartoum (International Crisis Group 2014: 23; Ofongo 2016: 146). Muhammed Ali and Khalid al-Barnawi (another Nigerian, and who later went on to assume leadership of a Boko Haram splinter group named Ansaru), became followers of bin Laden. Bin Laden gave approximately $3 million to Ali to establish a jihadist movement in Nigeria (International Crisis Group 2014: 23; Al-Risalah 2017: 19). On returning to Nigeria after the 9/11 attacks, Ali recruited Muslim preachers in Nigeria to become his deputies, including the then young Yusuf, who by that time had been in and out of various Salafi movements but found mentorship under Sheikh Ja'faar Adam.

In 2003, the Nigerian Taliban strove for self-exclusion of its members from mainstream society, which they viewed as corrupt, by migrating to rural parts of Yobe State 'in order to intellectualize and radicalize the revolutionary process that would ultimately lead to the violent takeover of the [Nigerian] state' (Isa 2010: 333). They regarded western education as apostasy and saw themselves as 'just individuals having similar ideology fashioned after the sacked Taliban regime in Afghanistan' (Murray 2004; Oropo 2004). Indeed, the Nigerian Taliban's encampment was also referred to as 'Afghanistan' by its members, some of whom were increasingly adopting a *takfiri* stance, and who launched small-scale attacks against Nigerian police stations (BBC 2004). The Nigerian government raided the community, killed Muhammed Ali and several dozen followers, after which the group dissolved, with some members fleeing Nigeria while others became immersed in the growing AQIM networks in the Sahel (Zenn & Pieri 2017: 292).

Yusuf fled to Saudi Arabia and was not to return to Nigeria until 2005, after a reconciliation with the state brought about by the then Borno State deputy governor, Adamu Shettima, and his old mentor Sheikh Ja'afar Adam. Yusuf is said to have given assurances that he was not involved in the violent uprising of the Nigerian Taliban and further swore not to espouse jihadist ideology. It was on these grounds that Yusuf's return to Nigeria was permitted. He settled in Maiduguri, the capital city of Borno State, where he started to preach and gather a band of followers around him. Yusuf initially kept to his word, distinguishing himself from the more militant ideology of the Nigerian Taliban by announcing that he believed it necessary to engage in *Iqamat al-hujja* – or "establishing evidence" – before declaring jihad (Yusuf 2007). His preaching was thus oriented towards convincing followers that the Nigerian government was corrupt and oppressive. In 2009, Yusuf published *Hadhihi Aqidatuna wa Minhaju Da'awatuna* ("This is our creed and the methodology of our propagation"). The book called for a return to practices based on the time of the prophet Mohammad, a so-called pristine age of Islam, in which the Qur'an, *sunna*, and *hadith* were the only guiding principles for Muslims. The text 'rejects democracy, secular constitutions and Western forms of governance, and seeks the gradual establishment of an Islamic state' (Barkindo 2017).

Yusuf's impassioned sermons were recorded on audio cassettes and sold to many who were eager to hear his message for Nigeria's future. By 2008 he had amassed enough followers around him to start building his own community of believers – a community that would be set apart from the Nigerian state by the devotion of his followers to a strict application of *shari'a* law. While this was a prominent feature of Yusuf's attempt to build his own 'state' or parallel society, there were also other features that may have appealed to those who joined. Abdu, one of my interviewees whose family member joined Yusuf's early community, told me that the benefits of the community included 'health care, Islamic schools, cash for members to start up small businesses, and arranged marriages.'[1] Abdu said that Yusuf encouraged his (male) followers to be successful in life, and many started small businesses such as shoe-shining stalls or bought motorbikes to be used as a taxi service. Yusuf demanded a 'portion of the profits to be paid back to him, and this money was then invested back into the community.' The issue of arranged marriages was of huge significance. As Abdu explained,

> in Kanuri culture, a person does not become a man until they have married, but it is impossible to marry without having money, because you have to pay a dowry price. Only older men who have wealth can afford that, and it is they who marry the young girls.

In effect, this left young men feeling emasculated, and Yusuf capitalized upon that by either paying the dowry price for his followers or completely by-passing the process, arguing that in his community of believers it was not necessary. He showed his followers in a literal way that, where the Nigerian state failed, there could be success if only people banded together and applied the *shari'a* to their own lives. The fact that Yusuf's community was relatively successful in northern Nigeria may have helped draw even more people to his cause, with many starting to see Yusuf as a teller of truth and as someone whose ideologies were favored by Allah.

Organizational structure

While insight into the early workings of the movement is difficult to come by, some detail is provided in *Slicing the Tumor*. It claims that Yusuf was able to establish centers of learning in 'Bauchi state, Kano state, Gombe and other places from the towns of northern Nigeria,' but that Borno State was 'the base and the directorate house for the brothers' (ISWAP 2018). Borno was the hub of Boko Haram's activities, and in 'most of its local governorates they had centers and agents, and in the capital of Maiduguri alone they had different schools and centers' (ISWAP 2018). The authors of this text outline five key operational hubs in the state for the movement's early activities, which were mostly centered around re-educating the followers of the movement to a version of Islam in tune with Boko Haram's worldview. At the very top of the system was the Ibn Taymiyyah Mosque complex[2] which Yusuf had built in the railway district of Maiduguri. The sprawling complex included schools, medical clinics, and gathering spaces. Yusuf gave his weekly Friday sermon here as well as administrated the activities of the other centers in Borno (ISWAP 2018). These centers included the Ta'ifa Mansura mosque located in the Unguwan Doki neighborhood which housed a council for *tafsir* – or exegesis – of the Qur'an every Friday night. In the center located in Millionaire's Quarter, Yusuf would give *tafsir* of the Qur'an every Thursday in Kanuri language, but it is claimed that he later had to transfer these lessons to the Ibn Taymiyya mosque for security reasons (ISWAP 2018).

It is difficult to comprehend the movement's scale at the time, the level of structure it had, and the impact that its activities were having in Maiduguri and the surrounding region. Here, again, *Slicing The Tumor* provides important insights, claiming that:

> By God's help, [Yusuf and his followers] established committees undertaking their affairs administratively and in terms of security, in order to educate the brothers, arouse their zeal and conform with the known circumstances, so it was as follows.
>
> (ISWAP 2018):

- *Majlis al-Shura* [Consultative Council]: comprising nine of the sheikhs, who joined the sheikh [Yusuf] and subsequently supported his *da'wa* [proselytization]. The sheikh would discuss with them to deduce matters that arose for the group, and issue orders appropriate to the interest of the brothers. He would also have them review his sermons, messages and books, to avoid the presence of a defect that the opponents could exploit to attack the group.
- The *walis* and *amirs* [district leaders] of the areas: deputies for the sheikh in the states in which they had their influence and centers, and they would refer to him new developments in the state that would pertain to security or fear, so the sheikh would help them or contact the *kafir* [infidel] government in order to investigate the matter, and likewise they would examine the work of the committees and would track them.
- Investigation committee: this would investigate all the committees, monitor the course of their works, and inform the *Majlis al-Shura* of them.
- *Da'wa* [Islamic Outreach] committee: comprising ulama [religious scholars] and students of *'Ilm* [knowledge], and those who serve them and accompany them in da'wa tours and travel to give lectures and *tafsir* of the Qur'an in Ramadan in different lands.
- *Hisbah* [moral accountability] committee: commanding what is right and forbidding what is wrong, like the stumbling block of shopping when we conduct prayers on Friday, preventing shouting during lessons, preventing adorned women from attending centers, and likewise undertaking the interests of the brothers and guarding their passengers from theft and organizing them in a way that does not narrow the road for pedestrians and passers-by.

The extent to which *Slicing The Tumor* may have exaggerated the reach of the movement is unclear, though it is certain that Boko Haram leaders will have tried to structure the movement in this way, also suggested by Onuoha (2012: 3), and which conforms with the ways in which other Islamist movements are structured. The movement was already forming the structure and blueprint for the creation of an idealized Islamic society, and this was most clearly expressed through the implementation of morality policing of the community through the *hisbah* committee. While Al Qaeda gave some initial seed funding to Boko Haram, *Slicing The Tumor* provides further details as to where money was coming from (ISWAP 2018):

- Economic committee: concerned with financing of the group, and providing the necessities to facilitate matters of *da'wa* through the following ways:
    - Financial donations offered by the rich of the people to develop the da'wa and its expenditure in God's path.

- Financial contributions paid for by the brothers in what they had accumulated themselves from their particular jobs and businesses.
- Agricultural resources that the group planted, harvested and then sold.

The above sources of funding were also highlighted by Onuoha (2012: 3), who adds that after 2009 'the group added bank robberies to its sources of funds for meeting different needs' which included 'helping the less privileged' and 'sustaining the widows of those that died in jihad.' In addition to all of this, Boko Haram leaders had established a militia 'concerned with the group's security and preventing them from doing anything that would stir up the government against them,' thus creating issues that would lead to problems with the state and its security forces. This militia was also tasked with uncovering 'spy cells, overseeing the works of the brothers and investigating their statements and lectures, then they would refer their names to the sheikh, so he would know of their position and beware of them' (ISWAP 2018). Another branch was 'confined to protecting the security of the sheikhs and guarding the centers, and trained secretly to bear arms and explosives' (ISWAP 2018).

Yusuf's discourse: challenging the status quo

Due to the expanding scale of Boko Haram in the early 2000s, politicians courted Yusuf, seeing him as an influencer and someone who could be used to win elections. Despite Yusuf dubbing the Nigerian system corrupt and immoral, Modu Sheriff, who was running for the governorship of Borno State, called on Yusuf and his followers to support him in his electoral race with promises of introducing *shari'a* and, if successful, renewing the moral climate of Borno (Abubakar 2017: 26). According to Hansen (2017: 562), Sheriff created a Borno State Department of Religious Affairs and appointed Alhajji Buji Foi (one of Yusuf's wealthy backers) as its first chairman. Once he came to power, however, 'Sheriff paid little attention to his promises' and 'effectively dumped' Yusuf and reneged on his promises regarding a strict interpretation of *shari'a* (Hansen 2017: 562). The consequence was that Yusuf and his followers denounced him as a traitor and began to subject Modu Sheriff to verbal attacks in public sermons.

Yusuf's message in 2008 was simple. His argument was that Nigeria is an illegitimate state, a construct born of western imperialism, based on misguided notions of democracy. Because of this, Nigeria had become corrupt and immoral:

> As written in Qur'an, there are certain things in this country [Nigeria] that are happening and they worry me a lot. First, you find that

infidels and unbelievers embezzle public funds, and assisted by local government chairmen, state governors and retired military officers, buy weapons and kill scores of Muslims. It is only when they are tired of the killing that the government will respond by sending in the police and military to keep the peace. Yet, when Muslims, overpowered by the anguish and the agony of what has happened to their brothers and sisters react, they are arrested by the military and police, while being branded terrorists.[3]

His solution was to call for a return to pre-colonial forms of governance based on *shari'a* law, as had existed in the Kanem-Borno Empire and in the Sokoto Caliphate. He argued that when the Muslim leaders of northern Nigeria abdicated their authority to rule to the British, they not only betrayed their own populations but also the sovereignty of Allah – something that Yusuf regarded as unforgivable and as the reason for the miserable state of northern Nigeria. Yusuf argued that the high levels of corruption and abuses against the population by their own government was a symptom of governance that had strayed from *shari'a* law. If only Muslims returned to governance based on the *shari'a* then these problems would start to disappear – just as they did when Usman dan Fodio ushered in the Sokoto Caliphate in 1804. Though a simplistic argument, its resonance cannot be overstated, and it shows the power of historical narratives in the formation and mobilization of Islamist movements. Yusuf's depiction of the destructive nature of colonialism is clear throughout his sermons, as demonstrated in Chapter 2.

The arrival of colonial powers in west Africa, and the lack of resistance (at least from Yusuf's perspective) from Muslim leaders, was the beginning of the downfall of Muslims in the region. This is because Europeans carved up the Islamic states that existed there, dividing the populations in arbitrary ways and merging Muslim populations with non-Muslims. To add to this, there was a push for democratization and the creation of constitutions for each of the states. For Yusuf, it was this fundamental shift away from Islamic governance to democratic forms of governance that opened the door for the downward spiral of society, the emergence of rampant corruption, and a state that was no longer interested in the development of its own population. Yusuf called upon his followers to reject democracy and to re-orient themselves to a stricter adherence of Islam, warning that failure to do so would prolong their misery.

Yusuf was initially both open and willing to engage with government, and especially so in Borno State, where he helped with the election of Governor Modu Sheriff. Boko Haram, due to its growing size and popular appeal among the population in Borno State in the early 2000s, was considered a source of potential votes. It is claimed that Sheriff even 'provided funding,

motorbikes and religious buildings before and after his election in 2003'
(Barkindo 2016) and also appointed backers of Boko Haram to positions of
governance. Yusuf may have believed that his influence with the Governor
would steer the administration in Borno towards implementing policies that
adhered to what Yusuf regarded as Islamically compliant. When this did not
happen, he started to turn against Sheriff and the entire concept of democratic governance. Quoting from Ibn Taymiyyah, Yusuf drew on the concept
of *taghut* – or idolatry – arguing that any form of governance derived from
a source other than the *shari'a* should be categorized as idolatrous. As far
as Yusuf was concerned, 'fidelity to the constitution of the Federal Republic
of Nigeria and subjecting oneself to the institutions created by it amount to
unbelief' (Muhammad 2014: 15). This was evidenced in a sermon Yusuf
gave in 2008:

> Allah revealed to us that to work under a secular government or col-
> laborate with it is a sin. It does not matter the type of work, every type
> of work under the secular government is a sin and in this case, there is
> no big or small sin, sin is sin. We just do not accept western civilization
> in anyway.[4]

Having said this, Walker (2016: 153) reports that right up to the eve of
the uprising of 2009, even with Yusuf's vitriol, he still 'believed that a deal
could be done with the state and Modu Sheriff would come around to their
uncompromising point of view.' All the while, however, Yusuf continued
to disavow any form of government employment and directly denounced
Governor Sheriff as a corrupt and immoral agent who was putting his own
interests above those of the people. Yusuf, in 2009, highlighted the failures
of Sheriff and the police and security forces, whom he accused of brutality
against the civilians they were meant to be protecting:

> But maybe if you [Governor Sheriff] stop cheating people, perhaps
> Allah will have mercy upon you. But look at you, you are the leader of
> democracy . . . and to add to that you are the leader of those flogging
> the people . . . Stop cheating people![5]

Yusuf was able to harness relevant social issues such as corruption and
state brutality to mobilize people to his cause. For those living in northeastern Nigeria who were experiencing the high levels of corruption and the
seemingly arbitrary nature of police brutality, Yusuf's words would have
stood out. As Yusuf's followers grew, his sermons became more incendiary.
In 2008, Yusuf outlined a jihadist vision for Boko Haram, albeit stating that
it was first important to gain strength before attacking:

What will stop them from insulting the prophet or killing the Muslims is jihad. But how are we going to carry out the jihad? Allah made me to understand that first and foremost, we must embark upon the preaching to Islamic reform. Then we will have to be patient until we acquire power. This is the foundation of this preaching towards Islamic reform. It was founded for the sake of jihad and we did not hide this objective from anyone.[6]

There can be no doubt as to which form of jihad Yusuf was talking about. This became even more alarming when, in the same speech, Yusuf advised his followers that if Muslims do not have the capacity to place someone of faith in power, 'then two things must be done.' Yusuf first called for all Muslims to 'proceed on *hijra*' and to 'search for the strength to succeed.'[7] He further stressed this point by stating that 'this is a duty upon all Muslims, none is excluded, both men and women. It is the law of Allah. There exists precedence both in Nigeria and in the world in general efforts to ensure that the law of Allah reigns supreme.'[8] It will not have been lost on Yusuf's followers that the call to *hijra* was the first step towards jihad against what was considered an illegitimate state – in much the same fashion as Usman dan Fodio. As Last (2014: 27) writes with regards to dan Fodio, underlying his actions was the 'model of the prophet, the account of whose *hijra* people knew so well. The Shehu [dan Fodio] was now taking the Sunna literally: if he did exactly what the Prophet had done, then Allah might give them success.' So too was the hope of Mohammad Yusuf.

While Yusuf's message was potent, it was not without challenge, and while challenges to Boko Haram could be expected from the Sufi brotherhoods and from "mainstream" Sunni Muslims, the challenges from within the Salafi strand of Islam were particularly hurtful to the group, especially as the leaders of Boko Haram positioned themselves within the Salafist context. This again was made clear in a sermon given by Yusuf in 2008:

We follow the ideology of the Salafists and any fatwa issued by a Salafist Islamic scholar, on it we stand. No matter how important an Islamic scholar is, we need to know if he is guided by Salafist principles before we accept such a scholar. We will accept scholars who preach and follow the Qur'an, the Sunna and the hadiths . . . Every teaching of a scholar must be supported by the writings and teachings of Salafist scholars.[9]

Yusuf was attempting to define his movement in line with Saudi Wahhabi orthodoxy, and as the gold standard for Islamic activism in Nigeria, this was a position that other Salafists in Nigeria would directly challenge. In 2007,

Yusuf's old mentor Sheikh Jafa'ar Adam went on record to 'denounce the group and warned that these ideologues were heading for violent confrontation with the state' (Walker 2016: 148). Adam further argued that Yusuf's opposition to 'western-style education would retard Northern Muslims' economic and political development' and painted Boko Haram as 'agents of outside interests, including Southern Nigerian Christians, the west, and foreign jihadis' (Thurston 2016: 13). Such accusations were to fortify Boko Haram's sense of exclusivism, 'making Yusuf and his core followers feel that they could no longer trust Salafis who defended Western-style education or government service; Yusuf, and later Shekau, came to anathematize and target Salafis who opposed Boko Haram' (Thurston 2016: 13). Adam was himself shot dead while at prayer in a Kano mosque, most likely by members of Boko Haram.

The turn to violence: 2009 and beyond

The decent into violence came amid increased tensions in Borno State as fears started to mount over the capacity of Boko Haram to act in violent ways. Governor Sheriff was alarmed at constant attempts by Yusuf and his followers to highlight him as a corrupt and ineffective politician, as well as by the more jihadist-oriented language that Yusuf was using in 2008:

> If you pay taxes, is it the country that benefits? Where exactly do they channel those taxes? They channel them into their private pockets. They are the country. Whenever you hear them saying, "help the country", they are calling for help for themselves. They want to rule over you and control you.[10]

The crisis point emerged around a new law that was implemented on January 1, 2009, which required all motorcycle riders to wear helmets. The law was not popular, and adherence to it 'never exceeded 20% at its highest, and by the end of February, two months after its effective date, virtually no one wore a helmet, as they do not to this day' (Hansen 2017: 563). The law, however, was applied against members of Boko Haram in June 2009, when the police entered into a confrontation with Boko Haram members in a funeral cortege for two members who had earlier died in an unrelated car accident. Some of the mourners were riding small 1100cc motorcycles, a typical form of transport among those not absolutely poor, though they were not wearing helmets. Governor Sheriff called on Operation Flush, a federal police program tasked to reverse Nigeria's epidemic of armed robbery and banditry. When Operation Flush police 'began harassing and attempting to detain bareheaded BH members, the mourners understood it as just one more act of harassment. Words were exchanged, threats issued, arrests made, shots fired, and nearly two dozen Boko Haram militants were dead or wounded' (Hansen 2017: 563). It was on this basis that Yusuf issued an open letter directly challenging the government and declaring jihad. This was also clear in a sermon given by Yusuf in 2009 in which he masterfully linked police practice over the helmet saga to brutality, arguing that injuries sustained from motorbike accidents are far less severe than injuries from police brutality:

> The security forces insist that bicycle and motorcycle riders must wear helmets so that in case of an accident they are protected from injury. Yet the torture ordinary people receive from the hands of the security forces is more than the injury people will sustain without helmets. Such injuries are even preferable to torture at the hands of the police . . . They cannot continue to treat ordinary people like donkeys. [11]

Yusuf went on to argue that no aspect of *shari'a* had been broken by his followers and that the actions from the police were disproportionate. Not missing an opportunity, he highlighted that the actions of the police should be viewed as part of the wider problem of corruption and impunity that stems from non-Islamic forms of governance. Yusuf also decried Governor Sheriff as a hypocrite, indicating that the thanks for Yusuf's support in getting him elected was repaid in the form of torture and killings:

> After all the law broken here is not the law of Allah, yet the police and security forces will torture and kill with impunity. What will the government achieve by killing and torturing its own people? What is the essence of this policy of security impunity? What have the people of this town done to the government to personally deserve this? What have they taken from the government coffers? . . . Is that what the governor will give back to the people; torture and killing, as a reward for their efforts in electing him? . . . How can you be elected to embezzle money and accumulate only for yourself and in addition, bring into the town a group of mad people [security forces] in the name of security. [12]

Following retaliatory attacks by Boko Haram for what they viewed as assaults on their own members, hundreds of homes, dozens of churches, and a number of police stations were destroyed in Maiduguri. In a cycle of escalating violence, Yusuf's Ibn Taymiyyah mosque was razed to the ground by the army, and hundreds of Boko Haram members, including Yusuf himself, were arrested and handed over to the police for interrogation by the army (Mustapha 2014: 150). One element that served to sustain Boko Haram's membership during this period, especially among ethnic Kanuris in north-eastern Nigeria, was hostility towards Nigeria's security forces after their brutal and indiscriminate crackdown on the group in Maiduguri in 2009 in which members as well as innocent bystanders were killed. That hostility 'was heightened by the fact that many of the security forces involved in the massacres came from outside the area and included Christians from the south of the country' (MacEachern 2018: 159).

Upon his arrest by the military, Yusuf was interrogated and asked about the workings of Boko Haram, as well as aspects of his own lifestyle. The interrogators were attempting to show Yusuf as a fraud – as someone who preached against corruption and exuberance – but was as deeply entrenched in the system as anyone else. This is seen in a segment of the interrogation:

Mil: How come you are eating good food . . . you look very healthy . . . you are driving good cars and wearing good clothes while you are enticing your followers to sell their belongings and live mostly on dates and water?

MY: That is incorrect. Every one of my members is living according to the means allocated to him by Allah. Everyone is different. Whoever you see driving a good car is because he can afford it and whoever you see living in want also means he doesn't have the means.[13]

It was also at this interrogation that Yusuf announced Abubakar Shekau as his official deputy and second-in-command – a move that would have unprecedented ramifications for the future evolution of the movement into a *takfiri* organization. The details as to how Yusuf went from the interrogation to being killed are murky, though it is without doubt that he was extrajudicially killed by the police. The BBC (2009) reported Nigerian police as claiming that 'Mohammed Yusuf was killed by security forces in a shootout while trying to escape,' with the same message of Yusuf's alleged attempted escape also coming from Governor Sheriff, though this could not be verified. Moreover,

> speculation as to why they [Yusuf and some of his prominent followers] were murdered in such a fashion without even the normal police "parading" has centered on what the movement's leaders could have said in open court about their support from and relationships with many prominent political figures including the governor.
>
> (Hansen 2017: 564)

Following Yusuf's killing, it was Sani Umar, not Abubakar Shekau, who initially emerged as a prominent figure and was to make the first speech outlining the movement's direction. Umar chastised those who called the movement "Boko Haram," stating that their ideology extended beyond opposition to western education to encompass all western ideas that were in opposition to Islam. Umar also took the opportunity to reach out to Boko Haram's followers, saying that Mohammad Yusuf did not die in vain, but rather as a 'martyr.' Umar in 2009 clarified the movement's position:

> We want to state clearly that Boko Haram is an Islamic revolution whose impact is not limited to northern Nigeria. In fact, we are spread across all the 36 states of the Nigerian federation, and Boko Haram happens to be a fraction of al-Qaeda which we align with and respect. We support Osama bin Laden and we shall carry out his command until the entire Nigerian nation is Islamized which is according to the will of Allah.[14]

Umar wanted to position Boko Haram as a force to be reckoned with and to situate it within wider international jihadism. He reiterated that Boko Haram had lost over 1000 members, whom he described as 'martyrs,' 'ambushed and killed by the wicked and callous members of the Nigerian army and police, who are mostly of the southern extraction.'[15] Umar went on to make six points, including that a jihad had started in Nigeria 'which no force on earth can stop,' that the movement would start to bomb southern cities, and that the aim was to 'make the country ungovernable, kill and eliminate irresponsible political leaders of all leanings, to hunt and gun down all those who are in opposition to the rule of sharia in Nigeria.'[16]

One point stood out, however, and that was Umar's call for all Muslims to rise up and join Boko Haram. Umar framed this struggle within the wider context of corruption in Nigeria, presenting Boko Haram, and its vision of carving out an Islamic state, as the only viable solution to rampant corruption and to political mismanagement:

> We summon all northerners in the Islamic territories and states to quit the followership of the wicked political parties leading the country, the corrupt, irresponsible, immoral, criminal and murderous political leadership and join the struggle for the law of Allah to be enshrined in the Nigerian society, where it will be corruption free, Sodom free and the security of lives and properties are guaranteed, with peace under Islam.[17]

Conclusion

While the extrajudicial killings of Mohammad Yusuf and other Boko Haram members in 2009 were not the first committed by Nigerian security officials, the fact that Yusuf was of a high profile in Nigeria allowed for the news to spread quickly, drawing outrage from his followers as well as wide-spread international condemnation. The adverse effects of the extrajudicial killings were highlighted in a report by Human Rights Watch (2012: 59), which claimed that such abuses 'created growing resentment in communities, making community members more unlikely to provide information that could help curtail Boko Haram' and that these abuses 'created more distance between the people and the government.' This is a factor that Boko Haram was able to capitalize upon, with the perpetration of abuses by the military playing into the hands of the movement. The 'Joint Task Force (JTF) through Operation Restore Order functioned like an army of occupation. Unable to distinguish Boko Haram members from unarmed civilians, they resorted to taking vengeance on the whole civilian population' (Muhammad 2014: 25). In essence this had the effect of creating a wedge between the security forces and the populations they were attempting to protect. The strategy of Boko Haram became to 'provoke the military by attacking and killing them, knowing full well that the military would kill defenseless citizens'; to the effect that by 2009 people started to 'openly affirm that Boko Haram, in spite of its excesses, was preferable to the military.'

After a brief period of minimal Boko Haram activity, the movement re-emerged in 2012 under the control of Abubakar Shekau and started launching attacks against its enemies. With the death toll mounting, Boko Haram attempted to pin the blame on the Nigerian government. The movement's spokesman, Abu Qaqa, in an interview reported in *The Guardian* newspaper (Mark 2012) on January 27, 2012, said:

> 'It is the secular state that is responsible for the woes we are seeing today. People should understand that we are not saying we have to rule Nigeria, but we have been motivated by the stark injustice in the land. People underrate us but we have our sights set on [bringing *Shari'a* to] the whole world, not just Nigeria. Poor people are tired of the injustice, people are crying for saviors and they know the messiahs are Boko Haram . . . People were singing songs in Kano and Kaduna saying: "We want Boko Haram." If the masses don't like us they would have exposed us by now. When Islam comes everyone would be happy," he said.

While clearly hyperbolic, the message is that Boko Haram was attuned to popular grievances expressed against the government and was masterful in re-framing these within an Islamist context. With the extrajudicial killing of their leader, Boko Haram became much more willing to use violence, increasingly in indiscriminate ways, in order to disrupt society and to achieve its objective of creating an Islamic state.

Notes

1 Participant Interview, January 13, 2014. Abuja.
2 Significantly the mosque was named after Ibn Taymiyyah, who is seen as the godfather of Islamist ideology due to his insistence on a strict interpretation and application of the *shari'a* and because he believed that 'the duty of Muslims to revolt against and change apostate rulers and governments in order to help re-establish a proper Islamic state' (Muhammad 2014: 21).
3 Yusuf, M. 2008. 'History of Muslims', in Kassim, A. and Nwankpa, M. (eds.). *The Boko Haram Reader: From Nigerian Preachers to the Islamic State*. Oxford: Oxford University Press, pp. 85–102.
4 Ibid.
5 Yusuf, M. 2009. 'Returning to the 'Quran and Sunna'', in Kassim, A. and Nwankpa, M. (eds.). *The Boko Haram Reader: From Nigerian Preachers to the Islamic State*. Oxford: Oxford University Press, pp. 159–164.
6 Yusuf, M. 2008. 'History of Muslims', in Kassim, A. and Nwankpa, M. (eds.). *The Boko Haram Reader: From Nigerian Preachers to the Islamic State*. Oxford: Oxford University Press, pp. 85–102.
7 Ibid.
8 Ibid.
9 Ibid.
10 Yusuf, M. 2008. 'Film', in Kassim, A. and Nwankpa, M. (eds.). *The Boko Haram Reader: From Nigerian Preachers to the Islamic State*. Oxford: Oxford University Press, pp. 77–82.
11 Yusuf, M. 2009. 'Returning to the 'Quran and Sunna'', in Kassim, A. and Nwankpa, M. (eds.). *The Boko Haram Reader: From Nigerian Preachers to the Islamic State*. Oxford: Oxford University Press, pp. 159–164.
12 Ibid.
13 Interrogation of Mohammad Yusuf by Nigerian Security Services, in Kassim, A. and Nwankpa, M. 2018. *The Boko Haram Reader: From Nigerian Preachers to the Islamic State*. Oxford: Oxford University Press, pp. 199–201.
14 Umar, S. 2009. 'Statement of Sani Umaru', in Kassim, A. and Nwankpa, M. (eds.). *The Boko Haram Reader: From Nigerian Preachers to the Islamic State*. Oxford: Oxford University Press, pp. 207–208.
15 Ibid.
16 Ibid.
17 Ibid.

4 "Western education is forbidden"

Introduction

On the night of April 14, 2014, almost 300 girls in the town of Chibok in the scorched plains of southern Borno, Nigeria's most northeasterly province, prepared to go to bed. The girls, all in their late teens, were in the dormitories of the Government Girls Secondary School, anxious that the next day they would awake to sit their final exams. As the girls slept, before the rising of the sun, the school was attacked with brutal force, and 276 of them were kidnapped by Boko Haram. The Nigerian military, according to Amnesty International (which the Nigerian government denied) had approximately four hours of advance warning of the attack but failed to reinforce the school (Amnesty 2014). The Government Girls Secondary School in Chibok is now a disarray of crumbling concrete amid an overgrown brush, a testament to Boko Haram's vision for western education in Nigeria. The attack served three purposes: the first was to reinforce Boko Haram's ideological point over the impermissibility of western education as well as emphasizing a theological point around the justification for the enslavement of non-Muslim women; the second was to capture young women as a means of demonstrating the strength and notoriety of the movement, as well as engaging in a tit-for-tat game with the Nigerian security forces who had previously arrested Boko Haram wives; and the third was to use the girls as bargaining chips for the release of captured Boko Haram fighters, a strategy that has been successful.

The world's media turned its gaze to Nigeria in the months after the attack, publishing images and footage of distraught parents crying while Abubakar Shekau delivered a video message promising to convert the girls to Islam or sell them into slavery (Shekau 2014). The targeting of women and children has garnered Boko Haram unprecedented media attention, notoriety, as well as infusing fear among the population (Bradford & Wilson 2013). The episode helped to highlight the precarious conditions of western education in northeastern Nigeria and solidified Boko Haram as a movement willing to act on its hatred of non-Islamic education, driven in part by its ideological belief that western education was usurping the hearts and minds of children. Ideology, and the specific emphasis on violently destroying western education, has functioned as a key driver of violence for Boko Haram. For the movement's leaders, western education stands for all that is wrong in the world – a system of knowledge which they perceive as morally corrupt and antithetical to Islamic teachings, leading young people away from a respectable way of life, their religion, and Islamic heritage. In February 2018, Shekau reaffirmed his movement's stance against western education, arguing that 'the one whose creed is to develop western education where infidels are trained is our enemy' (Haruna 2018a).

The Chibok girls are not the only women to be kidnapped by Boko Haram, with another example being the Dapchi girls, 111 of whom were abducted from their school dormitory in February 2018 by the Islamic State West Africa Province (ISWAP) faction of Boko Haram. The most interesting aspect of this situation was that, with the exception of one Christian girl, the girls were returned one month after their abduction. In essence, al-Barnawi's faction believes that the enslavement of Muslim girls is counter to *shari'a* law and that there was no justification for holding on to the girls. That the Chibok girls 'were largely Christian and the Dapchi abductees Muslim,' indicates why one set of girls was returned and the other kept (Bryson & Bukarti 2018). In both cases, however, women were directly targeted simply because they were in school.

Boko Haram started attacking schools in northern Nigeria with frequency in 2012, with 44 attacks that year resulting in 77 fatalities (START 2014). According to Human Rights Watch (2016) at least '611 teachers have been deliberately killed and a further 19,000 have been forced to flee since 2009' and 'more than 2,000 people, many of them female, have been abducted, many from their schools from the beginning of the conflict.' Between 2009 and 2015, attacks in northeastern Nigeria destroyed 'more than 910 schools and forced at least 1,500 to close. By early 2016, an estimated 952,029 school-age children had fled the violence' (Human Rights Watch 2016). This came on the back of a region already struggling to implement any form of education, with a rate amongst the worst in the world. The Nigerian Bureau of Statistics in 2017 noted that literacy rates in the northeastern states of Yobe and Borno were at 7.23% and 23.11%, respectively (Amzat 2017). The Chibok girls and their parents 'were supposed to be trailblazers – champions of a good education, but instead the fears of their community were confirmed. The kidnap proved to many that going to school was dangerous' (Leithead & Hegarty 2017).

Nigeria and especially the north of the country has had a long and contentious history with western education, and so opposition to it should not be seen as unique to Boko Haram but something they have amplified and used for a violent mobilization to its cause. Indeed, hostility to western ways of life stemmed back to the Hausa-Fulani aristocracy of the Sokoto Caliphate, who held that 'the teaching of western values perverted souls and compromised their piety, their humanity, and their sense of solidarity by promoting individualism and the emancipation of women, pushing back the age of marriage and thus the fertility of the Muslim masses' (Perouse de Montclos 2017: 27–28). Under the British colonization of Nigeria, northern emirs initially resisted sending their own sons to institutions of western-style learning, and instead the traditional madrassa-based Islamic schooling system, also known as *al-majiris*, prevailed. The British, governing through a system of indirect rule, allowed Islamic forms of education to continue much as before, even going so far as to restrict Christian missionary schools in the north 'in order to avoid undermining the influence of the Sokoto Caliphate, which had de facto become the best ally of London and the system of indirect rule to cheaply maintain order' (Perouse de Montclos 2017: 28). It was Britain's limiting of western education in the north, while pushing it in the south of country, that initially led to the educational disparities between north and south, though this solidified in the post-independence period due to the continuing distrust of western education in the north.

This chapter focuses on Boko Haram's ideological fixation on combating western education and western civilizational influences as a driver of the movement's violence in northeastern Nigeria and the wider Lake Chad Basin (LCB). The chapter will show that Boko Haram has drawn on the history of northern Nigeria to oppose western education since its inception, with this theme often central to its discourse. So prominent was this theme in the initial preaching of the movement it earned it the nickname 'Boko Haram.' The chapter will chart Boko Haram's evolution to violence against western education, from initially calling on parents to resist sending their children to western-style schools and urging graduates joining the movement to rip up their diplomas, to violently attacking schools, killing teachers and students, and abducting numerous schoolgirls. Ideological opposition to western education is rooted within the wider Islamist milieu and can be seen in groups ranging from the Taliban in Afghanistan to Tablighi Jamaat (Pieri 2015), but Boko Haram's actions have been at the most extreme end of the spectrum and have derived in part from local conditions in northern Nigeria and in part from the views of some Saudi scholars (Muhammad 2014: 17).

To understand Boko Haram's violent actions over education, we must first turn our attention to understanding the history and context of northern Nigeria itself – to the colonization of Nigeria by the British, the coming of missionaries, and the establishment of the first western-oriented schools in

the country. For Boko Haram, there is the perception that western education went hand-in-hand with Christian attempts to proselytize and spread
Christianity. Because of this, it sees western education as a Trojan horse that
will take children away from Islam and turn them towards a western way
of life – a life associated with loose moral values and an abandonment of
the belief in God's sovereignty. The chapter will show that Boko Haram's
arguments have been resonant in parts of northeastern Nigeria, especially
when combined with state corruption and nepotism. Yusuf articulated that
diplomas from western schools were useless and that public education was
a waste of time because it did not guarantee employment. His hope was
to 'eradicate the corruption instilled by a western model of education and
political organization that was considered anti-Islamic because democracy
aimed to give power to the people instead of God' (Perouse de Montclos
2017: 29).

The chapter ends with discussion of the Chibok girls, the majority of
whom were Christian, and who became a prized possession for Boko
Haram. The movement's brutal attack on the Government Girls Secondary School and the abduction of the girls brought into sharp focus Boko
Haram's beliefs about western education and gender-based violence that
is at the heart of its ideology and operations, while at the same time serving as an opportune strategic move through being able to use the girls as
bargaining chips in negotiations with the government. Footage of the girls
released by Boko Haram in propaganda videos will be analyzed, as will
Shekau's speeches relating to the girls. The Chibok girls became a show-
case for what Boko Haram stands for – first in receiving an Islamic education (provided by the movement) to counter their western knowledge and
then to accept Islam as their true religion, marry Boko Haram commanders
and be dutiful wives, and even be rewarded with servants of their own if
they remained loyal.

Colonialism and education in Northern Nigeria

Northern Nigeria has followed a different educational trajectory from the
south, and this is due to the vastly different historical trajectories of the two
regions. Prior to the arrival of the British in the mid-1800s, first through the
activities of the Royal Niger Company and then in the form of a colonial
administration, Nigeria as a territorial entity did not exist. In what is now
northern Nigeria, there were two Islamic states – to the west was the Sokoto
Caliphate, and to the east lay the ancient Kanem-Borno Empire, whose territorial might once reached into sizable parts of the neighboring Lake Chad
countries. Both states prided themselves on being Islamic in nature and, in
both, traditional forms of Islamic education flourished. Indeed, Borno, the

area in which Boko Haram has its strategic stronghold, was known as an epicenter of Islamic learning, with students seeking out instruction from Islamic scholars from across Sudanic Africa (Kollere 2007).

The south of Nigeria was made up of hundreds of independent kingdoms and tribes, each with their own language and distinctive cultures and religions. To the British, the Muslim north was seen as more civilized and structured, while the south was regarded as primitive. It is this dichotomy that influenced how the two different parts of what came to be known as Nigeria were governed. The north, through a policy of indirect rule, was given greater freedom to operate in keeping with Muslim traditions so long as it did not challenge British rule or contravene what Nigeria's first colonial governor, Lord Fredrick Lugard, called the 'laws of humanity' – an early conception of basic human rights. This was made clear in a political memorandum issued by Lugard in 1905:

> This application of English Law as the fundamental law was in the Supreme Court Proclamation of 1902 modified by an extremely important proviso, viz: that judges should take cognizance of native law and custom when not incompatible with humanity etc. . . . I emphasize once more that local proclamations supersede the Fundamental Law, so far as those matters are concerned.[1]

The result was that the colonial administration oversaw the implementation of Islamic law in a way that had not happened for some time, as the application of the *shari'a* had come to be somewhat lax by the late 1800s. Lugard was also emphatic that Muslim emirs should not be absorbed into British rule as direct agents of the British state but should be accorded special status on the basis of their traditional roles in Nigeria. In writing to his replacement as high commissioner, Percy Girouard, in 1908, Lugard, who was now in Hong Kong, stated that, 'Yes, I am emphatically in favour of ruling through the native chiefs, and not making them officials, and of allowing them a reasonable amount of pomp.'[2]

In the south of Nigeria the British implemented a policy of direct rule as a means of "civilizing" indigenous populations, though again the favored approach was to implement policies through existing elites. In southern Nigeria, Christian missionaries were allowed to flourish, and schools teaching a comprehensive education were established. In the north this was not the case. Christian missionaries were keen to expand their activities to the Muslim north, believing that Muslims, already being "half Christians" (perhaps due to Islam's monotheistic qualities and the special status of Jesus as a prophet), were ripe for conversion. By 1897, as Ayandele (1966: 125) argues, the Church Missionary Society (CMS) 'began looking forward to the subjugation of northern Nigeria, which they hoped would, as in southern Nigeria, open the door to the Christianization of northern Nigeria.' Though cautious of the impact that Christian missionaries could have on British rule in northern Nigeria, at first Lugard was permissive of their activities and aided in the establishment of missionary stations in a number of northern towns. Roads were secured to allow missionaries to travel, and according to accounts from Bishop Tugwell, from Jebba to Zaria 'we have been welcomed everywhere by the people.'[3] To reassure the northern emirs, Lugard promised that the colonial administration in Nigeria would not interfere with Islam, which is quite different from saying that missionaries would not be allowed in the north.[4]

Yet, while Lugard was not initially opposed to the activities of missionaries in the north, his primary goal was to secure successful British rule, which at times was made difficult by the brash and overly zealous activities of some of the missionaries. One such example is crystalized in an exchange of letters in 1908 between Girouard (who replaced Lugard as governor in 1906) and Lugard:

> I fear none of us, though admiring the pluck and single-mindedness of Miller have any patience with his fanaticism or the tactlessness of [Bishop] Tugwell . . . Their thoughtlessness for our difficulties culminated at Zaria, where the Bishop, assisted by Miller, openly baptized a mallam in the river, and in the presence of a large but fortunately not hostile crowd. Orr [The British DA] was not even informed of the proposal. I immediately notified Miller that any such ceremonies must take place within the missionary precincts, and informed Lord Elgin of the occurrence of this most unfortunate blunder.[5]

The problem was that Muslims in northern Nigeria would come to associate all missionary activities as attempts to convert Muslims to Christianity. This was to have an impact on education such that even many of the emirs would find 'excuses' not to send their sons to government schools. The activities of Christian missionaries were to be restricted, and education was allowed to remain in a traditional and Islamic format. The colonial records present the friction between the desire of missionaries (predominantly Protestant) to aggressively evangelize the Muslim population of northern Nigeria, including through inserting Christian doctrine into mission schools, and the desire of the colonial administration to keep religion out of the picture. This is captured in the letter from Sir Percy Girouard to Lord Lugard in January1908:

> Miller promised not to proselytize during school hours, but felt himself free of any such promise out of school. The result has not been good,

and personally I am strongly opposed to the Church Missionary Society having any educational functions amongst the Mohammadans. I can only support the policy of a former chief, Lord Cromer, who positively forbade Christian missionaries in Northern Nigeria or Mohammadan provinces of the Sudan, while welcoming them in the pagan South.[6]

In effect, the British colonial administration, out of fear that the missionaries would damage relations between the administration and the local population in the north, as well as out of a notion of respect for Muslim customs, stymied missionary schools in the north. Peter Tibenderana (1983: 525) postulates that British officials overplayed anxieties by the emirs 'and merely used [them] to conceal the anti-missionary attitude harbored by many British political officers.' His argument is that the cause of educational stagnation in northern Nigeria during the colonial era was not based on the emirs' 'alleged dogged conservatism' nor that British educational policy was palatable to the emirs because of its alleged aim of maintaining the status quo. Rather, Tibenderana (1983: 533) argues that the emirs' interests and those of the British in the realm of education were at variance.

> Whereas the former demanded more schools and better education, which they knew would enable their subjects to be appointed to positions of responsibility in government, which were held by Europeans and people from southern Nigeria – a process which, in their view, would eventually shorten British rule – the latter worked for its longevity by restricting educational expansion.

Irrespective of what motivated education policy in northern Nigeria during the colonial period, the reluctance to allow western-oriented schools was retained through Lugard's administration as well as that of his successor, Percy Girouard. In 1909, however, Sir Hasketh Bell replaced Girouard, and he was less keen on restricting the activities of missionaries in the north. Bell gave the CMS permission to start working in Kano in 1909, but until 1920 they were unsuccessful due to disapproval from the Colonial Office in London, who viewed missionary activities as damaging to British relations in the region (Danmole 1996: 215). Provincial schools were also established, though they never became as popular as the traditional form of Islamic education. The colonial administration, keen to alter the balance, made innovations, starting with the inclusion of Islamic instruction alongside the more secular curriculum (Danmole 1996). The schools were mainly accessed by the children of northern elites, and a widespread suspicion remained over fears of a hidden agenda to evangelize Muslims.

Qur'anic schools continued much as before, but this ultimately condemned many in the north to a form of education that was not well adapted
to the modern period and led to a large literacy gap between the predominantly Christian south and the predominantly Muslim north. Islamic education in northern Nigeria is also known as the *almajiris* system. The system
comprises boys and young men from the ages of 5–21 who have left home
to live with a *mallam* – or Islamic religious scholar – to study the key texts
of Islam, including the Qur'an and *hadith*, the Sunnah of Mohammad, and
the Arabic language. Most learning is done by repetition and recitation.
Hannah Hoechner (2014: 67) describes these schools as

> largely beyond the state's purview and regulatory interventions, the teacher
> receiving no salary but living off the support given by the local community,
> the alms given in exchange for his spiritual services, the contributions of
> his students, and supplementary income-generating activities.

It is well known that the majority of *mallams* do not themselves have formal
qualifications and are often 'products of the *almajiri* system'. Because of the
strictly Islamic nature of the *almajiris* system, the students who go through
this education are left ill prepared for work in the wider (more secular)
world, and many turn to petty trade, farm work, and in many cases begging.

By 1952, both Muslim elites and the colonial administration recognized
that Muslims in the north were being let down by the *almajiris* system.
A report by P.H.G. Scott (1952: 8) found that Islamic education was failing
because of an 'over-emphasis upon the study of the Arabic language and
the transmitting of religious instruction into a routine school subject. In
others it is undoubtedly due to the poor quality of the persons employed as
teachers.' The intention of the regional government, according to Scott, was
to take action to 'improve the quality of the teachers and to provide by the
expansion of the School for Higher Arabic Studies at Kano, for the raising
of standards of all teachers of Islam, including those from unrecognized
Koranic schools.'

Something should also be said about education for girls in northern Nigeria, which often reflects on the types of opportunities that are afforded to
women as well as their capacity to join the labor market. Bilkisu Yusuf
(1991: 90) argues that Islam in northern Nigeria affects 'women's spatial
freedom, and therefore access to education and politics, more profoundly
than in the south.' The neglect of women's education in northern Nigeria
is not a new phenomenon and predates Usman dan Fodio's jihad of 1804.

> Nana Asmau's [dan Fodio's daughter] example as an educator notwith-
> standing, minimal literacy skills and religious tenets were taught to

women – just enough to allow them to say their obligatory prayers. When religion has been taught to women, Islamic injunctions on women's rights nevertheless have been distorted by local traditions to favor men.

(Yusuf 1991: 92)

It is even more tragic, therefore, that Boko Haram has targeted the ire of its fanaticism against female students enrolled in western schools.

This desire for the north to maintain a distinct Islamic education has continued into the modern period, and even where more comprehensive forms of education have been implemented, the state of education has remained stagnant. This point is stressed by Hoechner (2014: 69), who argues that 'educational disadvantage in northern Nigeria extends far beyond the *alma-jirai*, as the low secular school enrolment rates for girls, or the poor achievements of even those children who do attend secular school, attest.' This severely disadvantages Muslim communities, who are often left without the core skills to function in modern integrated economies.

"Western education is forbidden"

Boko Haram is avidly against the establishment of western education for Muslims, and indeed this is a main facet of the movement's ideology. It was once a rite of passage for new members of the movement to tear up or burn their certificates from western schooling they had received – a gesture that marked their rupture with the established social order. According to Barkindo (2018: 57), Boko Haram see the edifice of western civilization as constructed on three fundamental pillars. These are 'western education, Judeo-Christian traditions, and democracy.' It is the collaboration between these that has led to what Shekau describes as 'globalization and the modern world order' (Barkindo 2018: 57). Shekau argues that the west uses education to infiltrate Muslim minds and destroy Islam. Western education for him is the foundation of immorality and all that is evil in the world. In 2009, Shekau issued a warning stressing the urgency of abandoning western schooling, claiming that failure to do so could result in being excluded from paradise in the hereafter:

Western education is the most nonsensical form of education. If you have a son in school, you should immediately withdraw him. If you are a secondary school student, you should withdraw immediately without wasting any time. If you are up to level four, or any year in the university, you should quickly withdraw, withdraw, withdraw. If you are hoping for paradise, withdraw. I swear by Allah: western education is a lie and a deception.[7]

Shekau, in 2011, argued that western education is the gateway to moral corruption and decay of Muslim societies, aptly linking this to globalization as a destructive force:

> Followers of western education have usurped our hearts with a philosophy and method of thinking that is contrary to the demands of Allah. They have destroyed our style of life with a system that has not been instructed to us by the Prophet. Today the government rejects the Qur'an, the Prophet and the religion of Allah in public life. It replaces these with the concept of a new world order, globalization; a new system of directing world affairs. How can you as a Muslim live in this new world order and gain paradise? This is precisely what we the Muslim *ummah* is fighting. This is what we have declared we do not want.[8]

Boko Haram leaders argued that such systems of education must not only be rejected but must be replaced by Islamic ones where Allah is the means and the goal. Mohammad Yusuf stressed this in an interview with the BBC in 2009 (Boyle 2009) before his death:

> There are prominent Islamic preachers who have seen and understood that the present western style education is mixed with issues that run contrary to our beliefs in Islam. Like rain. We believe it is a creation of god rather than an evaporation caused by the sun that condenses and becomes rain. Like saying the world is a sphere. If it runs contrary to the teachings of Allah, we reject it. We also reject the theory of Darwinism.

Boko Haram, like other Islamist movements, claims to be concerned that the impacts of western education detract from the attainment of life in paradise in the hereafter. As such, if taken at face value, the movement is one that is driven by notions of salvation and in searching for ways to navigate to salvation in an increasingly changing and globalizing world. For Boko Haram, the response has been one of violent resistance. The accusation is that western nations through the use of soft power in the form of education have created a global context in which Muslim ways of life have been destroyed. In this context, Shekau argued, 'Allah is excluded from the values of western education' and that anyone who has adopted a western mindset 'roams the street like a hyena, trying to convince others to become faithless and godless.'[9] This is presented in stark contrast to the forms of government that existed in northern Nigeria prior to colonialism, where in both the Kanem-Borno Empire and the Caliphate of Sokoto, *shari'a* was integrated into the fabric of the state. Boko Haram leaders argued that western education went as one with colonialism, especially with Christianity and the drive by Christian missionaries to convert Muslims to Christianity. The argument is that western education is a tool to Christianize Muslim children and to divorce them from their religious and cultural heritage. Even though the record shows that the British colonial administration stopped the proliferation of missionary schools in northern Nigeria, and in fact did much to protect Muslims from external influences, this did not stop Mohammad Yusuf from propagating the narrative. This is a narrative that places the failings of the Muslim north firmly on the shoulders of outsiders and an argument that often resounds with an already frustrated population:

> This system of [western] education was imposed upon us by the Europeans. Anyone who reads history, except a fool, knows that the Europeans handed over this form of education to the missionaries. The missionaries included into the curriculum of western education the belief system and values of Christianity . . . Allah revealed to us that to work under a secular government or collaborate with it is a sin . . . We do not accept western civilization in any way. If it is intellectual development that can advance religious education, we can do it without embracing western education and civilization . . . We refused to accept the form of education that originated from the western world. We also reject the western construction of the concept of nation that excludes the law of *Shari'a*. We reject forms of work and all kinds of jobs based on western concepts and ways of doing things.[10]

Despite this strong focus on the moral perils of western education, according to one of my interviewees, it is the more practical side of Boko Haram's argument on this topic that has more potency among the population: 'Western education is frustrating because it gives you certain expectations, and these expectations are rarely met in the northeast.'[11] Explaining what was meant by this, the interviewee continued:

> You leave these schools with the expectation of a good job and a better quality of life, but people can't get good jobs unless you know someone. It is not education that matters but who you know, and so the problem is corruption.

Another interviewee stated that 'western education lets communities down.'[12] Pressed to go further, he said 'because people just can't get jobs so they become useless to their families. Where does western education lead us to? If we can't get jobs what's the point of it?' Yet another interviewee noted that

> western education is meaningless when you are jobless. The children of western education become divorced from the land, cash that could have been spent on crops is wasted, and what for? The child can't contribute to the traditional economy anymore and if they then can't get an office job it leaves them bitter and meaningless.[13]

Boko Haram fuse contemporary practical concerns around education with a narrative that is based in history. They argue that at the point of Britain's arrival to northern Nigeria, "true" Muslim leaders, horrified by the notion of western education, banded together in a violent jihad to fight against the implementation of western schools:

> When they [Muslim leaders] heard that they [the British] had brought western education, they said: 'By Allah we will not accept it!" . . . They waged jihad against this western education yet today you are forcibly enrolling your son into western education!? And seeing it as an epitome of civilization? Our forefathers waged jihad against western education – against the Europeans.[14]

While this is a distorted historical narrative, it served the purpose of moving the fight against western education from the realm of discourse to that of physical violence, backing it up with what Boko Haram leaders believed to be historical legitimacy. Physical attacks against schools started in July 2009 at the very point that the discourse had shifted to this more violent narrative, though did not become an entrenched tactic until after 2012. In addition to the ideological strand of combating western influence, there is also a more strategic goal of attacking schools in that Boko Haram 'insist they are attacking schools in retaliation for JTF [Joint Task Force] atrocities' (Muhammad 2014: 28). According to Boko Haram's spokesman in 2012, Abu Qaqa: 'We attacked schools because security operatives are going to *Islamiyah* schools and picking on teachers.'[15]

The attacks on schools and teachers, and the killing or abduction of pupils, forced many schools to close down. Though some are reopening, many children, according to Elizabeth Pearson, have not returned due to continued insecurity and fear of attack.[16] Interestingly, before his extrajudicial execution, Mohammad Yusuf was interrogated by the Nigerian police, who explicitly asked him to defend his views on education. Their argument was that Yusuf and his followers were hypocrites – that they enjoyed the outputs of western education such as computers and technology while all the while blasting how evil such education can be. The military interrogators argued that the Qur'an stipulates that Muslims should strive to seek knowledge, and Yusuf's response was revelatory:

Yusuf: That is correct, but not the kind of knowledge that goes against the teachings of Islam, the one and true religion of Allah. Any kind of knowledge that goes against the teachings of Islam is prohibited by the almighty, such as sorcery and magic. These are knowledge but Allah has forbidden it. Shirk [neglecting duty]; polytheism or associationism, the practice of associating something with Allah as partners is knowledge but Allah has forbidden it; astronomy is knowledge but Allah has forbidden it . . .

Mil: At your place we found computers, syringes . . . are all these not products of knowledge?

MY: They are purely technological things, not Boko . . . and Westernization is different.

Yusuf's reasoning, though perhaps strategic, is not uncommon amongst Islamists, who do not claim to reject western knowledge simply because it is western, but rather on the basis of whether or not it conforms to Islamic teachings. What distinguished Boko Haram is that it has been willing to take its concerns with western education to the most extreme levels, burning down schools, killing students and teachers alike, and abducting schoolgirls for sexual slavery.

The Chibok schoolgirls

Although Boko Haram has been fully active as a violent jihadist movement since 2011, it was not until 2014 that the movement came to international notoriety with the abduction of the Chibok schoolgirls. The images of the Chibok girls clad in dark burkas, downcast and forced to recite Islamic prayers, reverberated across the world. The movement had sent a clear message that it was firmly opposed to western education in northern Nigeria and willing to use lethal force in order to achieve its ends. The reality is that Boko Haram had been attacking schools, killing teachers and pupils, and abducting school girls since 2012, though the scale of the Chibok attack was unprecedented. The tragedy was augmented by a gesticulating Shekau, in a propaganda video released a month later, swearing that he would convert the girls to Islam, marry them off to Boko Haram commanders, or sell them into sexual slavery on the open market:

Any female who has attained the age of 12, I will marry her off. Any girl who has attained the age of 9, I will marry her off, the same way they

married the mother of believers, the daughter of Abubakar [Moham-
mad's father-in-law and Islam's first Caliph following Mohammad's
death] Aisha to the prophet Mohammad at the age of 9 . . . I am the
one that captured your girls and I will sell them in the market. I have
my own market for selling people. Allah commanded me to sell the
girls.

Shekau justified his actions within the context of Islamic history,
namely that girls could be married off as young as the age of nine, based
on Aisha's reported age of marriage to Mohammad.[17] Indeed, the Islamic
State of Iraq and Syria, in issues 4 and 5 of *Dabiq*, its English-language
magazine, cited the kidnapping of the Chibok girls as justification for
their own sexual enslavement of Yazidi women. Boko Haram have used
women and girls for the purposes of 'procreation, killing machinery,
domestic duties, and human shields' (Oriola & Akinola 2018: 604). While
the Nigerian government was slow to act and seen by many as ineffective, a campaign on Twitter emerged under the hashtag of #BringBack-
OurGirls and was endorsed by Michelle Obama, then First Lady of the
United States. The website dedicated to #BringBackOurGirls demands
that the 'Chibok schoolgirls abducted on 14 April, 2014 be rescued by
the government. Improve government's accountability to Nigerians on
security issues, particularly in the northeast.'[18] Some progress has been
made (see ahead), though 112 girls (as of June 2018) were still missing,
and some were featured in propaganda videos claiming that they do not
want to return.

The first images of the kidnapped schoolgirls were released as part
of a Boko Haram propaganda video shortly after their abduction in the
early days of May 2014. The 27-minute footage is stamped with the logo
of a pair of crossed Kalashnikovs, a black flag, and an open Qur'an.
The girls were shown dressed in Islamic garments, sitting outside under
a tree and repeating Qur'anic verses, while two girls in the back held
up the black flag of Boko Haram inscribed with the words "There is no
God but Allah, Mohammad is his Prophet." The setting is clearly one
of an outdoor African-style Islamic school. It is interesting that the first
video of the Chibok girls presented them in a classroom setting – in
essence they retained their status as schoolgirls – but the form of education being received was very different. Depicted sitting in orderly lines
wearing black and grey colored veils, they repeated the first chapter
of the Qur'an by rote – a method popular in Islamic schools. That the
girls were reciting the first verses of the Qur'an shows that their "re-
education" under Boko Haram was underway and that they had started
from the beginning. The one and only text for the "classroom" was
likely to be the Qur'an.

The propaganda video served as a powerful symbol for Boko Haram's message, for the movement was (at least in appearance) putting into practice what it preaches. That is a return to education based on a fully Islamic system and on the traditional method of schooling that had been established in the north of Nigeria prior to Britain's colonization of the country. For Boko Haram it is a superior system, believed to nourish the soul and prepare an individual for salvation.

In the same video footage, Shekau, with a gun strapped across his chest, gesticulated and in an animated manner explained why the girls were taken. Using the language of liberation, he first explained that, contrary to what people were saying, the girls had not been kidnapped but liberated through their conversion to Islam, which he emphasized seven times in just the opening segment to his speech. Shekau explained that the capturing of slaves is allowed under Islam, but when slaves convert to Islam, they take on the status of believers equal to other Muslims. For Shekau, these schoolgirls, most of whom are Christian, were captives of a corrupt and faithless system, attending schools that did not teach Islam, serving to inculcate in the girls a form of debased and immoral fantasy: an education that stemmed from a Christian colonization of Nigeria and which was serving to divorce the girls from what Boko Haram sees as the Islamic heritage of northern Nigeria. Shekau secondly explained that Boko Haram was giving the girls a chance at real freedom – the freedom to become Muslim women – some of whom he claimed had converted already, while others not. The girls are dressed as Muslims, they chant from the Qur'an and will be expected to behave as Muslim women – or at least what Boko Haram leaders imagine to be the role of Muslim women.

Given this strong ideological thread in Shekau's discourse, and the lengths he went to as a means of conveying a better future for these girls as Muslim women, it seems strange that he also signaled a willingness to enter into negotiations for their release – at least for the ones that had not converted to Islam:

> We will not free them until you free our brothers you imprisoned in Borno, Yobe, Kano, Kaduna, Abuja, Lagos, and even Enugu. By Allah, they have imprisoned our brothers all over the country. There are those that have been imprisoned for five years, so they have not seen their wives or children . . . You captured our children and families, killing our brothers.[19]

The demand was clear, Boko Haram would release those girls who refused to convert to Islam in exchange for captured Boko Haram members, and as such suggests that the abduction of the girls was as much strategic as ideological. Boko Haram leaders on several occasions repeated their willingness to release the girls in exchange for Boko Haram members held by the Nigerian government. Indeed, calls to release female hostages date back to 2012, when Nigerian security forces arrested and detained more than 100 women and children, including Shekau's own wives. The arrests were 'not unusual in themselves' but were significant because the 'deployment of such practices to strike at the heart of Boko Haram through Boko Haram's female family members in turn had a significant impact on Boko Haram's strategy' (Zenn & Pearson 2014: 47).

Despite international outrage and a sustained campaign from Nigerian citizens to see the safe release of the girls, little traction was made. On April 14, 2015, the one-year anniversary of the kidnappings, Nigeria's then president-elect Muhammadu Buhari said that he could not promise that the girls would be found. A few months later, in September 2015, Buhari, still under pressure to secure their release, raised the possibility of releasing Boko Haram prisoners in exchange for the girls, and in December he said he was willing to negotiate with any 'credible' Boko Haram leader, but only if proof was provided that the girls were still alive. In essence he was taking Boko Haram at its word – that the movement would release at least some of the girls in an exchange of hostages. On August 14, 2016, Boko Haram released video footage of 50 of the girls, all of whom were in dark veils, sitting together, and some of whom were crying. One of the girls was holding a baby, indicating that at least some of the girls had given birth to children of their own. One of the girls, identified as Maida Yakubu, was allowed to speak and addressed her message to the parents of Chibok (McClean 2016):

> There is no kind of suffering we haven't seen. Our sisters are injured, some of them have wounds on their heads and bodies. Tell the government to give them [Boko Haram] their people, so we can come home to you . . . We are all children. We don't know what to do. The suffering is too much. Please try. We have been patient. The only thing that can be done is to give them their people so we can go home.

The video was intended to put pressure on the Nigerian government at a time when Boko Haram's position was weakening. Islamic State had removed Shekau from the leadership of Islamic State West Africa Province (ISWAP), and the Nigerian government was making strides in reclaiming territory lost to the movement. The warning in the message was that any attempts to attack Boko Haram could result in injury or loss of life to the girls, and that the only way to secure their safe release was to release captured Boko Haram members. The video also demonstrated that at least 50 of the girls were alive and in the possession of Shekau's faction of the

movement. Through all of this women were targeted for 'instrumental purposes, as none of those captured . . . had any direct involvement in the conflict' (Zenn & Pearson 2014: 47)

Behind the scenes, the Nigerian government, along with the government
of Switzerland and the International Red Cross, was negotiating with Boko
Haram. The first breakthrough came in October 2016, when 21 of the girls
were released in exchange for four jihadist prisoners. In May 2017, another
82 girls were freed in exchange for five Boko Haram commanders as part of
the ongoing negotiations. Over time, however, reports emerged that some
girls were fully indoctrinated, that some had assumed positions of leadership
in the movement, acting as "den mothers" training and disciplining other
abducted girls into the movement's expectations. Many of the girls were
married to Boko Haram commanders, and a few claimed refusal to leave
the movement. Charmaine Pereira (2018: 261) notes there exists 'considerable heterogeneity in women's conditions of life under Boko Haram.' In the
case of Aisha, the wife of Mamman Nur, it is described how 'she enjoyed
respect, influence, and standing within Boko Haram, with abducted women
as her slaves' who did everything for her, including washing and babysit-
ting. Pereira (2018: 261) describes that though Aisha was kidnapped, she
was not forced to marry her husband and instead was 'courted for several
months and received numerous gifts' and that Nur even divorced one of his
other wives at her request.

On January 14, 2018, Shekau released a further video of the Chibok
schoolgirls, along with some policewomen that had been captured (Haruna
2018b). He said:

> The Chibok schoolgirls, who have gone through the western education,
> are today following the book of God, because they have come to under-
> stand that the constitution is not the right path but a deception. They
> have now realized that your laws in Nigeria are not good for them . . .
> The Chibok girls that have become Muslims, and got married peace-
> fully, are even calling on the parents to come accept Islam . . . And we
> call on the parents of the Chibok girls that have become good Muslims
> to accept our ways and be part of us. You have become our in-laws by
> the virtue of your daughters marrying us.

Shekau's speech, though provocative in goading the parents of the Chibok girls and calling them his 'in-laws,' was also revelatory of Boko Haram's continuing ideological fixation with western education and what it
considers western values. Shekau notes that through re-educating them in
an Islamic fashion, they have come to understand that the Nigerian constitution is a 'deception' and that they have embraced Islam. Not wishing to

miss the chance to solidify this message, Shekau allows one of the school-girls to speak, who reiterates his message:

> Oh you our parents in Nigeria, I call on you to repent and worship Allah. We are very happy because we have found a way to Worship Allah. It is Him alone that we worship here; do repent and come to worship your creator. We pity you our parents that you have not accept the ways of Allah. You are only worshipping the country and its constitution. What a pity. It is ignorance.

It is of course possible that over years in captivity some of the girls came to adopt Boko Haram's ideology, perhaps initially out of fear or from the need to survive. Ahmad Salkida, a Nigerian journalist who has had access to senior Boko Haram members, commented that 30 out of the remaining 113 Chibok girls in custody of the insurgent group are still alive. In a report by Sahara Reporters (2018b), he is quoted as explaining that a leading member of Boko Haram

> clarified that 15 girls were still alive, and that two other Boko Haram cells within the larger group brought additional information, clarifying the earlier information, that there are another 10 girls available to another cell. Outside of the 15 and 10, another five among the girls are also alive.

The mass kidnapping of young women as bargaining chips for the release of Boko Haram commanders and members is one that continues, but which has also been affected by the ideological splits and fracturing within Boko Haram. A prominent example came in February 2018, when Boko Haram militants most likely allied to the Islamic State faction of the movement stormed the town of Dapchi in Yobe State, seizing 110 girls from the Government Technical College. One aspect that the militants did not consider was the religion of these girls, all but one of whom turned out to be Muslim. Therefore, the girls, with the exception of the Christian girl among them, were later released. According to Zenn (2018c), when the militants

> brought the girls from Dapchi to Abu Musab al-Barnawi's base near Lake Chad, al-Barnawi then demanded their release (except for the one Christian girl who could be "enslaved" according to his ideology). Since the kidnapping itself was unacceptable, al-Barnawi did not demand ransom or prisoners in return for their release.

This clearly distinguishes al-Barnawi's faction of Boko Haram from the one operated by Shekau, and highlights al-Barnawi as someone who places greater emphasis on following Salafist injunctions regarding who could and could not be enslaved.

The tactic of kidnapping young girls increases the level of press coverage and notoriety of the movement, keeping it at the forefront of attention, but also demonstrates the capacity of the movement to act in such ways, despite continued claims by the Nigerian government that Boko Haram has been defeated. The lesson learned is that because the government of Nigeria has been willing to negotiate with Boko Haram over the release of schoolgirls in exchange for Boko Haram members, the tactic will likely continue into the future and disproportionately affect Christian girls.

Conclusion

The harrowing situation of the Chibok and Dapchi schoolgirls shows that Boko Haram is willing to act violently to disrupt western education in northern Nigeria, to destroy schools, to kill teachers and students, and to abduct countless girls and boys. It is clear that opposition to western education and western values such as democracy and constitutionalism have proven to be drivers of violence. Boko Haram, through the case study of the Chibok girls, has also shown (at least in their propaganda videos) that, beyond its violent actions, it is serious about the education of women – albeit in a way it believes to be in accordance with *shari'a*. Its propaganda videos went to great lengths to show that the movement was re-educating the girls and that over time the girls had come to accept Islam, marry Boko Haram commanders, and even take up Boko Haram's cause themselves. At the same time, the case of the Chibok girls shows Boko Haram to be a strategic organization as much as it is ideological. Boko Haram leaders were willing to put strategy over ideology in their willingness to exchange the girls in return for captured Boko Haram commanders.

The question of education simmers at the top of the Nigerian cauldron and formed an integral part of the 2015 General Election campaign. The then incoming President, Mohammadu Buhari, recognized the prime importance of bolstering education in northern Nigeria as well as combating the associated problems of corruption and radicalization. As Buhari (2015) wrote:

> My government will first act to defeat it [Boko Haram] militarily and then ensure that we provide the very education it despises to help our people help themselves. Boko Haram will soon learn that, as Nelson Mandela said, "Education is the most powerful weapon which you can use to change the world.

The irony of the matter is that many Islamists, too, see education as a powerful weapon which can be used to change the world, and it is for that reason that battles over the education of children can become so vigorously fought. Indeed, Nigeria is only one example in which battles over the nature of education have been raging. Some of the most pronounced clashes have occurred at the intersection of education, religion, and science. Religious fundamentalists across all faiths have had a particular interest in shaping the institution and curricula of education. Education has a lasting impact on young people and has the power to form and influence how lives are lived. For some there is a belief that the impact of education goes even further, affecting one's very soul and salvation. It may sound a strange argument, but it is a common concern across the board for those with absolutist religious beliefs.

Education has become a battlefield, especially in postcolonial settings, as fundamentalists push back against secular state control. While the role of the state in deciding the educational curriculum has always been contested, what is changing now is that some are willing to take lethal action to counter what they perceive as the negative effects of secularism which they also regard as the bedrock of western education.

Notes

1 Lugard, F. 1905. *Political Memoranda*. MSS Lugard 55/2 ff. 1–114.
2 Lugrad, F. 1908. Letter from F. Lugard to G. Percy. April 12. MSS BRIT.EMP. S.63 ff. 152–163.
3 C.M.S. G3/A9/01. Tugwell to Baylis. February 19, 1900.
4 C.M.S. G3/09/03. Memorandum of interview with F. Lugard. July 25, 1912.
5 MSS Brit EMP. S. 63 ff. 164–205; Letter from Sir Percy Girouard to Sir F. Lugard January 25, 1908.
6 Girouard, P. 1908. Letter from Sir Percy to Sir F. Lugard. January 25. MSS Brit EMP. S. 63 ff. 164–205.
7 Shekau, A. 2009. 'This is Our Creed'. Trans. Barkindo, A. in Kassim, A. and Nwankpa, M. (eds). *The Boko Haram Reader: From Nigerian Preachers to the Islamic State*. Oxford: Oxford University Press, pp. 145–146.
8 Mallam Abubakar Shekau, Nigeria, October 28, 2011. www.youtube.com/watch?v=eQY4GLtzLdU.
9 Shekau, A. 2009. 'This is Our Creed'. Trans. Barkindo, A. in Kassim, A. and Nwankpa, M. (eds). *The Boko Haram Reader: From Nigerian Preachers to the Islamic State*. Oxford: Oxford University Press, pp. 145–146.
10 Shekau, A. 2011. 'A Message From Shekau'. Ocober 28. www.youtube.com/watch?v=eQY4GLtzLdU
11 Participant Interview, January 15, 2014. Abuja.
12 Participant Interview, January 16, 2014. Abuja.
13 Participant Interview, January 20, 2014. Abuja.
14 Nur, M. 2009. 'Returning to the Quran'. Trans. Kassim, A. in Kassim, A. and Nwankpa, M. (eds). *The Boko Haram Reader: From Nigerian Preachers to the Islamic State*. Oxford: Oxford University Press, p. 153.

15 *Daily Trust*, February 29, 2012.
16 Elizabeth Pearson, personal communication, December 22, 2018.
17 While this is the commonly accepted age of Aisha when married to Mohammad, there are some varying accounts (Bloom & Matfess 2016: 114).
18 See, www.bringbackourgirls.ng (accessed: June 15, 2018).
19 Shekau, A. 2014. 'Message About the Chibok Girls', in Kassim A. and Nwankpa, M. (eds.). *The Boko Haram Reader: From Nigerian Preachers to the Islamic State*. Oxford: Oxford University Press, pp. 311–317.

5   Construction of a caliphate

Introduction

In August 2014, Abubakar Shekau triumphantly declared the establishment of an 'Islamic state' (*dawla islamiya*) in the parts of northeastern Nigeria that were under the control of Boko Haram, in effect creating what the group perceived as a caliphate.[1] With this, Boko Haram accomplished its long-term goal to "carve out" territory for a polity to be ruled under strict *shari'a* law in northern Nigeria, a return to what they believed mirrored Usman dan Fodio's caliphate (1809–1903). The objective of seizing territory in which *shari'a* could be implemented was prevalent in Mohammad Yusuf's sermons and remained a constant aim of the movement. After the announcement in 2014, Boko Haram continued to annex numerous towns in Borno, Yobe, and Adamawa States (Pieri & Zenn 2016: 66; Thurston 2018: 225; Varin 2016). By January 2015, Boko Haram was in control of some 20,000 square miles of territory in northeastern Nigeria (land approximately equivalent to the size of Belgium) while also perpetrating attacks in northern Cameroon, southeastern Niger, and southwestern Chad. Shekau's *baya*, or pledge of allegiance, to Abubakar al-Baghdadi, the self-styled caliph of the Islamic State, in March 2015[2] highlighted Boko Haram's position among internationally recognized jihadist movements and, at the same time, marked the climax of the movement's territorial control. Although the Nigerian military, in concert with the militaries of neighboring countries, was able to reclaim much of the land seized by Boko Haram in the lead-up to the Nigerian general and presidential elections of 2015, Shekau's formal announcement of an 'Islamic state' and his pledging of allegiance to the Islamic State in March 2015 demonstrated the seriousness of Boko Haram's message (OCHA 2017).[3]

The aim of this chapter is to explain how Boko Haram came to occupy such large swaths of land, threatening the stability of Nigeria and wider security of west Africa. The chapter draws on primary sources and emerging research on the topic to argue that a catalyst for the formal occupation by Boko Haram of land in northeastern Nigeria was linked to the reintegration of a Boko Haram splinter group – Ansaru – into the fold of the movement. The argument, most prominently made by Jacob Zenn (2018a), is that Al Qaeda in the Islamic Maghreb (AQIM) provided training for the Nigerian militants in Boko Haram who broke away from the group in 2011 and formed Ansaru in 2012. These militants then reintegrated into Boko Haram in 2013, bringing with them their tactical knowledge and an impetus for kidnappings, suicide bombings, and conquest of territory.

As well as providing a perspective on how Boko Haram was able to establish territorial control over a portion of land in northeastern Nigeria, the chapter will also present an analysis of how Boko Haram attempted to govern that land. Through the use of video footage taken by a Boko Haram videographer for the group's own record keeping and made available (at least in part) by Voice of America (VOA), a picture emerges that, while Boko Haram was not yet ready to take on the governance aspect of territorial acquisition, there were serious attempts to impose a strict Islamic moral order throughout the areas it controlled. This was best exemplified through harsh rules regarding dress codes for both men and women, the segregation of men and women at public gatherings, and the public implementation of Islamic law through *shari'a* trials, with punishments taking place as an enforced "community" event.

The chapter links Boko Haram's drive to create a pure Islamic order with the wider and largely failed push for the expansion of Islamic law in northern Nigeria, implemented in part in 1999. Many northern Nigerians gathered publicly in 1999 calling for an implementation of *shari'a* law, believing that this would be the most effective solution to society's ills. Exhausted by 'endemic corruption, and poverty, regular, struggling citizens put their faith behind politicians who promised them a new era of justice energized by the idea of *shari'a*' (Eltantawi 2017: 200). Similarly, Boko Haram, at least in its early phases, was able to tie its own ambitions for territorial control to existing concerns festering in society, with the promise that its version of Islam was the solution. In both cases, attempts at reviving *shari'a* did not live up to popular expectation.

The Ansaru factor

One important question asked about Boko Haram is that of how the movement managed to gain control of so much land in northeastern Nigeria in such a short space of time. In essence, what were the driving factors behind Boko Haram's turn of fortune in 2014 that allowed for territorial acquisition? Jacob Zenn (2018a) argues that the catalyst is to be found in the reintegration of Ansaru members into Boko Haram's fold, an assertion that has been contested by Higazi et al. (2018). Ansaru, which is a shortened version of the group's official name, *Ansarul Muslimina Fi Biladis Sudan*, meaning 'Vanguards for the Protection of Muslims in Black Africa,' first emerged as a distinct organization in January 2012 in the northern city of Kano. It is likely that Ansaru split off from Boko Haram due to 'displeasure at Boko Haram's style of operations, which it condemned as inhuman and damaging to Muslims, in particular the attacks against Muslims and innocent non-Muslims' (Pantucci & Jesperson 2015: 25). Indeed, in Ansaru's own proclamation of its formation, it argued that 'the foundation of Ansaru is the result of injustices, the plethora of violent and barbaric actions against the Muslims of this country [Nigeria].'[4] In addition, four goals were articulated:

1. Preaching the straight path and raising the consciousness of the people
2. Protection of the lives and property of Muslims
3. Quick response and retaliation against any unjust or terroristic action against Muslims
4. Return of glory and nobility, which was during the time of the caliphate, to the Muslims, just as it was during the caliphate of dan Fodio.

These goals are important because they distinguished Ansaru from Boko Haram, which was becoming increasingly violent and indiscriminate in its attacks. The goals also grounded Ansaru within the ideological framework of al Qaeda, which has traditionally emphasized a more moderate approach to Muslims. To better understand how and why Ansaru's reintegration with Boko Haram was able to spur the acquisition of territory in northeastern Nigeria, it is the relationship with al Qaeda, and specifically to AQIM, that must be examined. The process of becoming an 'affiliate of al Qaeda is long and formalized, and that process was never finalized with Boko Haram' and as such 'it never reached the level of a formal, public merger or affiliation' (Thurston 2018).

Having said that, what is clear is that relationships between al Qaeda and Boko Haram at first, and later on with Ansaru, did extend beyond just ideological links. AQIM initially provided Boko Haram with some financial support and training for a number of its members. This emerged in comments made by Abdelmalek Droukdel, then the emir of AQIM, who confirmed that in 2010 AQIM and Boko Haram were in communication and that AQIM was willing to support Boko Haram. Zenn (2018a: 7) writes that Droukdel also wrote to Abubakar Shekau promising 'the equivalent of $250,000, weapons which are "in abundance", and training for "waves" of Boko Haram fighters.' Despite this type of willingness to invest in Boko

Haram, AQIM was to become disenchanted with the movement, not least because of Boko Haram's turn towards indiscriminate violence against the civilian population of Nigeria, including Muslims, which Al Qaeda viewed as outside the permissible tactics of jihad.

In *Slicing the Tumor*, it was claimed that Ansaru was compelled to split from Boko Haram due to Shekau exhibiting signs of extremism, including:

> Denying the excuse in ignorance in *kufr* [infidels] absolutely, and *takfiring* [apostatizing] the Muslims dwelling in the land of *kufr* as individuals, deeming their blood and wealth not to be sacrosanct for protection, and the group's method in conveying the *da'wa* [Islamic propagation] and dealing with the masses changed fundamentally, and Shekau treated those in the group close to him with tyranny and unfairness.
>
> (ISWAP 2018)

Because of this, AQIM wrote to Shekau advising him to return to a more orthodox interpretation and application of Islam, but Shekau did not listen, causing Boko Haram to split 'into divisions.'

It is here that the relationship with Ansaru becomes important because the members who split from Boko Haram to form Ansaru had a closer affinity with AQIM. It is those members who also had the tactical know-how and capability for carrying out sophisticated attacks and who closely mirrored Al Qaeda in terms of ideology and tactics such as the kidnapping of foreign nationals and attacks on western targets (Comolli 2015: 103). Zenn (2018a: 8) noted that many of Ansaru's hostages worked for engineering companies,

> which were a typical AQIM kidnapping target, and its claims resembled al Qaeda narratives, such as calling for the release of a female al Qaeda web administrator from prison in Germany . . . and an end to France's military intervention in Mali.

Ansaru was instrumental in initiating the use of suicide bombings in Nigeria, and while Ansaru did not claim these attacks, they were masterminded by Mamman Nur and his associates who were aligned to Ansaru, though not formally part of it, as they feared retribution from Shekau if they formally split from Boko Haram (Zenn 2018a: 8).

Zenn (2018a) highlights that members of Ansaru had skills that were not exhibited in Boko Haram operations during the period of the split and that when some of those Ansaru members reintegrated into Boko Haram in 2013, this tipped the balance in Boko Haram's favor in terms of carrying out more sophisticated attacks which then allowed the movement to take control of territory in the northeast of Nigeria. Zenn reached this conclusion through an analysis of attack data to show that Ansaru was carrying out large-scale attacks during the period of separation from Boko Haram and that Boko Haram's attacks only reached a similar level of sophistication after the reintegration occurred in 2013. The majority of suicide bombings from 2011 to 2012 were in Nigeria's Middle Belt, which was Ansaru's strategic area of operation, but from 2013 both suicide bombings and kidnappings 'migrated to northeastern Nigeria and the neighboring border regions of Niger, Chad, and Cameroon' (Zenn 2018a: 12). This analysis is tempered by Higazi et al. (2018: 2016), who argue that the 'identity of the suicide bombers was hardly ever revealed.'

Another important factor in the development of relationships between Boko Haram, Ansaru, and AQIM is the Islamist takeover of cities such as Gao, Kidel, and Timbuktu in northern Mali. While this is also challenged by Higazi et al. (2018: 207), Caroline Varin (2016: 72) argues that in Timbuktu, 'AQIM ran a sophisticated training camp for multinational terrorists, the majority of whom were Nigerians' and that over a nine-month period, 'hundreds of Boko Haram members stayed at these camps where they learned to fix Kalashnikovs, and launch shoulder-fired weapons.' Varin (2016: 72) acknowledges that there is some dispute over the details of these camps but is clear that there was an 'exchange of communications between the leadership of Ansaru and AQIM: in February 2013, Ansaru flyers were discovered in AQIM commander Mokhtar Belmokhtar's compound after he fled Gao.' The Mali takeover is important because it is the stage where the reconciliation between Ansaru and Boko Haram likely took place, thus allowing for a stronger and more experienced Boko Haram to emerge (Africa Confidential 2013).

The question then arises over why Ansaru would have wanted to reintegrate with Boko Haram after so explicitly criticizing Abubakar Shekau and his tactics of indiscriminate attack, which they considered to be outside the standard conventions of jihad. One explanation is that Khalid al-Barnawi, the leader of Ansaru, had become desperate. For example, 'in March 2012, Nigerian counterterrorism units killed al-Barnawi's deputy, Abu Muhammed, and several of his *shura* (council),' and at the same time the Ansaru cells 'responsible for the kidnappings of the British and Italian engineers in Kebbi in May 2011 were also broken up,' while on top of all of that, 'Shekau was ordering the killing of Ansaru members' (Zenn 2018a: 14). Because of those factors, 'Al-Barnawi may have feared for his own life because in January 2017 an Ansaru leader wrote that Shekau had also tried to kill al-Barnawi in his car' (Zenn 2018a: 14). The end of Islamist rule in Mali caused the fracturing of ties between Ansaru and AQIM as AQIM leaders fled to north Africa, and this may have spurred Ansaru to look back at Boko Haram. While the narrative around the role of Ansaru remains contentious in academic debates, with Zenn (2018d) responding to critiques, the consequences were that the integration of those Ansaru members coincided with the time at which Boko Haram was able to launch campaigns to capture territory in the northeast of Nigeria.

The push for the acquisition of territory by Boko Haram in northeastern Nigeria started in the spring of 2013 after the integration of Ansaru and with the raiding of military barracks, the first of which was in the town of Monguno. This raid, as well as others that Boko Haram carried out in Borno State, were important because they 'eliminated the Nigerian military presence from large swaths of territory in northeastern Nigeria and allowed Boko Haram to conquer territory' (Zenn 2018a: 20). By January 2015 Boko Haram was in control of 20,000 square miles of territory in northeastern Nigeria while also having the capacity to carry out brutal attacks and suicide bombings in Cameroon, southeastern Niger, and southwestern Chad (Pieri & Zenn 2016: 67).

While evident that reintegration of Ansaru members with sophisticated knowledge of combat was important to Boko Haram's success, there was also a tactical underpinning that united the leadership of Boko Haram and Ansaru – that was the drive for the annexation of territory as rooted in historical precedent and which created a deep resonance with the want to (re)create a caliphate in northeastern Nigeria based on the legacy of Usman dan Fodio. This is clearly seen in discourse from Boko Haram and Ansaru. Boko Haram sought to establish its state based on the model of Usman dan Fodio, but rather than doing this in the Hausa States where dan Fodio operated, it operated within the boundaries of the historic Kanem-Borno Empire, the traditional homeland of the Kanuri.

This overlaying of Boko Haram's territory within the historic boundaries of the Kanem-Borno Empire was remarkable and more than just coincidence. Dan Fodio's heartland of Sokoto, in contrast, remained outside of Boko Haram's orbit. This

> represents the main paradox of Boko Haram: it seeks legitimacy and inspiration from dan Fodio, the Fulani founder of the Sokoto Caliphate, in order to create its own caliphate, but its leaders and members are predominantly Kanuri operating in the areas of the former Kanuri-led Kanem-Borno Empire.
>
> (Pieri & Zenn 2016: 68)

This does not mean that Boko Haram should be viewed as a "Kanuri Movement" or that it even perceives itself in this way. Instead Boko Haram from 2013–2015 saw itself as a contemporary manifestation of dan Fodio's jihad, using the same core arguments to attack rival Islamic leaders, albeit in the heartlands of Kanuri territories.

Becoming a part of the Islamic State

The specifics of how Boko Haram came to align itself with the Islamic State and the consequences of this on the movement will be discussed at greater length in the next chapter. Important here is that by 2015 the Islamic State had grown to become one of the most notorious jihadist movements on the planet, drawing thousands of recruits from around the world to its operational stronghold in Syria and Iraq, and was promising to revive a golden age of Islam that would usher in the end times (Wood 2015). Uncompromising in its ideology, brutally violent in its tactics, and making strides to establish a 'caliphate' in the Middle East and beyond, it is easy to see why some in Boko Haram were attracted to aligning themselves with the Islamic State. In March 2015, Shekau, as emir of a reunified Boko Haram, pledged allegiance to Abubakar al-Baghdadi, the self-styled caliph of the Islamic State. In his oath, Shekau said:

> We announce our allegiance to the Caliph of Muslims, Ibrahim b. Awad b. Ibrahim al-Husayini al-Qurashi [Abubakar al-Baghdadi] and we will hear and obey him in times of difficulty and prosperity, in hardship and in ease . . . We [Boko Haram] pledge allegiance because there is no cure to the Muslims' disunity except the caliphate. We also call Muslims to join us in this goodness, because it would enrage Allah's enemy. By Allah, our gathering under one imam is more detrimental to enemy morale than their gaining victory in the battlefield.[5]

This pledge was recognized by the Islamic State, and Boko Haram officially became the Islamic State's West Africa Province – ISWAP. The name was significant because it gave Boko Haram a more regional focus, and although this did not materialize, it was to position ISWAP as the hub of jihadist activity for the Islamic State in the region. On the face of it, Shekau had ushered Boko Haram into its golden age. By March of 2015, the movement was in control of and attempting to govern physical territory in the northeast of Nigeria, and a relationship with the most notorious jihadist movement of the age had been cemented.

The situation, however, was far more complex, and the pledge came at a time when Boko Haram was starting to incur losses. Through 'hitching its wagon to the rising star of the Islamic State and its brand, Boko Haram could claim that its version of Salafi-jihadism has global legitimacy, a propaganda move designed to offset its territorial setbacks' (Thurston 2016: 24). The internal dynamics of the pledge to Islamic State also show that the push for alignment with the Islamic State did not come from Shekau, but rather from Mamman Nur and Abu Fatima. These two senior members of Boko

Haram, who had largely been sympathetic to the Ansaru splinter group in the past, "compelled" Shekau to pledge allegiance to the Islamic State because, according to Nur in 2016, 'it is obligatory to pledge allegiance to the Caliph once he appears in the world.'[6] Moreover, according to Nur, Shekau feared that his not pledging allegiance to al-Baghdadi would lead Abu Musab al-Barnawi, Mamman Nur, and Abu Fatima to break away just like they had as part of Ansaru. Shekau, who had never formally joined al Qaeda, may not have wanted to formally join the Islamic State either, but instead to have mutual recognition, so as not to have to sacrifice his authority to another leader.

Governing Boko Haram's 'caliphate'

Boko Haram's declared 'caliphate' was centered around the town of Gwoza in Borno State, which was captured by Boko Haram and brought under its control in early August 2014. Recognizing the importance of spectacle, Boko Haram was quick to name the town as the capital of its Islamic state, and in a visual display hoisted its black flag over what was at the time the residence of the emir of Gwoza, leaving no doubt as to the shift of power in the town. Abubakar Shekau triumphantly proclaimed, 'Thanks be to Allah who gave victory to our brethren in Gwoza and made it part of the Islamic State.'[7] With Gwoza in hand, Boko Haram went on to capture 'Bara, Buni Yadi, Marte, Gamboru Ngala, Dikwa, and a number of smaller towns on the Cameroonian border,' as well as the large town of Bama (Campbell 2014). Boko Haram swiftly renamed the towns – Gwoza became *Dar al-Hikma* (Abode of Wisdom) and Mubi became *Madinatul Islam* (City of Islam) (Kassim & Nwankpa 2018: 321).

The clearest indication of Boko Haram attempting to create its own state with a system of governance was in the replacing of emirs, or traditional rulers, in the cities and towns it captured. By 2015, the emirs of Gwoza, Bama, Damboa, and Dika had been replaced. Traditionally in Borno, the emir is responsible for appointing all other village heads and is thus in a position to exert great influence.[8] To Boko Haram, the traditional emirs did not represent legitimate Islamic rulers, but rather those who sold out to what was seen as the corruption of the federal government in Abuja. The emirs that Boko Haram installed were expected to start implementing the movement's vision of an Islamic state, and placed in those positions were allies of the movement. In the strategically important town of Bama – the second largest town in Borno after the capital Maiduguri – Mohammed Danjuma, a Boko Haram member 'popularly known for his brutality' was installed as the new "emir" (Abusidiqu 2014a). In the town of Dikwa – about 30 miles from Maiduguri – Boko Haram announced the installation of Bulama Yaga as emir. The interesting point about Yaga is that he was not an ethnic Kanuri (the predominant ethnicity of those in Boko Haram), and this exemplified that Boko Haram was more concerned with seeing religiously orthodox Muslims (or at least those that followed Boko Haram's version of Islam) in positions of power, irrespective of ethnicity (Abusidiqu 2014b).

The declaration of a northeastern Nigerian Islamic state marked a noteworthy turning point in Boko Haram's evolution, namely having to deal with the practicalities of providing governance in captured towns and cities while at the same time having to continue fighting with government troops and disgruntled populations for control of those areas. Given the complex security situation in Borno State, and the fact that Boko Haram is a closed and hostile group to "outsiders," it is difficult to present a complete picture of what life was like under Boko Haram's territorial control. Analysis has had to depend on the testimony of those who experienced life in the 'caliphate' as well as through the use of video footage taken by Boko Haram itself. While video footage cannot be considered a full representation of the everyday experience of life under Boko Haram rule, it does present a valuable segment that contributes to the overall picture The video footage comes from a series of recordings taken from the hard drive of a Boko Haram laptop, containing over 400 video files and roughly 18 hours of footage. The hard drive was delivered to Voice of America (VOA), where it was determined that the videos came from a Boko Haram laptop that had been captured in a Nigerian military raid (VOA 2017a).

The footage[9] shows an arid, desert landscape in which oxen still pull carts and camels are used for transportation. Women who appear in the footage (often in the background) are dressed in colorful *chadours*, and many of the men shown have adopted a mixture of Islamic and western dress. Boko Haram flags, which are modeled on the Islamic State's flag, and logos appear frequently throughout the footage and very prominently during any form of *shari'a*-based punishment such as public executions or amputations, at which there is always a large crowd spectating (Pieri & Zenn 2018). According to VOA (2017a), the recordings were made in late 2014 and 2015. This was a period of expansion by Boko Haram in northeastern Nigeria which culminated in the physical takeover of land and the carving out of Islamic territory.

A trial in the town of Kumshe

One of the video segments shows a tribunal that Boko Haram set up in the northeastern town of Kumshe to judge, punish, and execute those whom the movement accused of moral crimes. The video shows the people of the town gathered around a grassy area. Two men hold up a white Boko Haram banner with black Arabic script that says, 'There is no God but Allah,' and beneath, also in black script but enclosed in a circle or seal, are the words, 'Allah's messenger Mohammad.' Some Boko Haram members hold AK47s, and the majority of the crowd are men, mostly in Islamic dress, although a few appear in western style t-shirts. A judge in a white *shalwar-kemeez* – a garment composed of loosely fitted pants with a long over-shirt –black waistcoat, and white turban asked three men who are shown sitting on the ground if they accepted his verdict of guilt for dealing in drugs – the penalty for which is death. All three men denied the accusation, and each time a denial was made, the crowd cried out 'Allah Akbar!' There were other men, a larger group, shown on camera, sitting behind the three accused of drug dealing. These men were accused of using drugs, and as such would be lashed in public but not executed, though if caught again they would face death. Each of those men was lashed 10 times, and with each lash the crowd chanted 'Allah Akbar!', perhaps fearing that failure to participate verbally in the punishments would put their own lives in danger.

Boko Haram seemingly showed no discrimination in terms of the age of those being lashed, and the group included an elderly man and a young boy wearing a ripped purple t-shirt, though the vast majority fell somewhere in between. Footage was taken of the boy being lashed, and once the punishment was completed, he stood up and prostrated in a prayer-like fashion towards Boko Haram's banner. The footage of men being lashed lasted for around 30 minutes, and at times Boko Haram commanders picked out men in the crowd to carry out the lashings on behalf of the movement, truly making it a form of "participatory justice." When this finished, only the three men accused of drug dealing remained sitting on the ground. Each of these men had his hands tied behind his back. The first man was carried by his shoulders and legs by two Boko Haram members and placed in the middle of the grassy area. While lying on his stomach, in his blue robes and with his face in the grass, he pointed his two index fingers upwards toward heaven, a gesture that is commonly perceived to open the gates of heaven for those about to enter. A Boko Haram member approached him from behind with an AK47, pointed it at the man's heart (through his back), and shot him. The crowd erupted into a chant of 'Allah Akbar!' The other two convicted men, in turn, walked calmly and lay down beside the first man, and they too were shot dead.

Once all three men had been killed, the camera panned out, and the crowd prostrated in a prayer-like fashion, while a senior Boko Haram member announced that God's justice was implemented and that sin was being eradicated: 'We have delivered Allah's justice! All of those people here are those who spread mischief on earth and not only earth, but in an Islamic state.' The camera also showed a sizable group of women – all veiled in *niqabs*, and many young girls in colorful *chadours* – who were segregated from the men, but it is clear that all members of the town, male and female, young and old, were required to participate (even as spectators) in the public administration of "justice."

A judgment on homosexuality

Boko Haram has long decried homosexuality, with it being a fixture of many of sermons, the topic often being integrated with democracy and western education. For Boko Haram, both democracy and western education are seen as paths that lead to homosexuality, or at least an acceptance of homosexuality, something that Boko Haram regards as toxic and as damaging to the moral fabric of society. In a lecture by Mamman Nur in 2009,[10] he stated that:

> The systems of western education are all evil; you cannot take female children to a boarding school to become lesbians with fellow females. The females are now even engaging in marriage [with each other]. The government of Nigeria has now given them permission. If a man wants to marry another man they have given them permission. So will you not destroy this government of prostitution?!

It is not surprising therefore that once in control of territory, Boko Haram would make it a point to carry out punishments for those convicted of homosexuality, and this is clearly demonstrated in the footage that emerged from within Boko Haram's territory. At a public gathering, Boko Haram prepared to execute two of its own members on the charge of homosexuality. A man dressed in a blue *shalwar-kemeez*, with a green head covering and an AK47 strapped across his chest, wearing a black wristwatch and holding a microphone, announced that he was a messenger from Shekau:

> My brothers I am here to relay a message from our leader, our highest leader, and fellow brothers in Islam. Allah has tested us with hypocrites from amongst us. Any religion in which you stay peacefully with unbelievers in not from our prophets.

Through this statement the messenger admits there are 'hypocrites' within the ranks of Boko Haram, showing that sinful activity may be found anywhere, and also reiterates one of Boko Haram's main claims, that Islam is not a religion of peace, especially when it comes to 'unbelievers.' It also highlights the two men convicted of homosexuality as now falling into the camp of un-believers through an act of *takfir* – or excommunication – thus making their execution permissible.

Boko Haram set the stage for the execution in what was the central square of the town. A grassy area was cordoned off and had the appearance of a rink with a crowd of spectators on all four sides. The crowd is shown as being strictly segregated, with men and boys in one area and women and girls in another. The two accused men were forced to lie on the ground. Both these men were in western clothing – trousers and what could be described as trendy shirts. They were in stark contrast with members of Boko Haram, who were all dressed in an Islamic fashion, as were most members of the crowd watching the execution, including many children. Both men were shot in the back, through the heart, and killed.

The fact that Boko Haram carried out such a brutal punishment against two of its own members (though there is no clear evidence that the two men really were members) is highly significant because it demonstrates willingness to apply the law equally, irrespective of affiliation. In this sense, their ideological fixation with administrating the full extent of the law stems back to similar examples from Usman dan Fodio, on whose caliphate Boko Haram claimed to have based its short-lived state.

Dan Fodio's emphasis on *haad* (the implementation of violent punishments prescribed in Islamic law) was a way of establishing the seriousness of the Islamic tradition, and a method that would penetrate human psychology to its deepest core. This seriousness in turn would help to 'offer no-nonsense solutions to Hausaland's deep social and moral problems' (Eltantawi 2017: 41). In order to illustrate this dan Fodio is said to have quoted a saying of the prophet Mohammad regarding a woman who had stolen:

> That which annihilated those that came before you is that they carried out the *haad* punishment on the common man, setting aside the shari'a, and I declare by my hand that if Fatima [the prophet's own daughter] did the same thing that her hand would be cut.

Through this, dan Fodio admonished Muslims for 'failing to mete out *haad* punishments as consistently as they should. Even if Fatima herself, Mohammad's daughter, had stolen, she too would have her hand cut off.' (Eltantawi 2017: 63). That the law should be applied in all its severity, without compromise, to all Muslims, is something that Boko Haram was trying to show through the conviction and execution of two of its own members accused of homosexuality. As important as ideology is to the core leadership of Boko Haram, the application of Islamic law through the use of public spectacles could also have been as much about intimidating local populations and maintaining order through fear.

The use of force and "downtime"

While much of the footage from within Boko Haram's territories showed the movement attempting to implement Islamic law, other aspects that were covered included negotiating with village elders, downtime for Boko Haram foot soldiers in their camps, and preparations for and engagement in military-type activities. In one of the segments, Boko Haram foot soldiers were shown assembled before the start of a battle, with AK47s in hand and with RPGs, receiving a pep talk from one of their commanders in both Arabic and Kanuri languages. The young men were told:

> Allah says the best of the martyrs are those who fight in the front. They are the ones that do not turn back until they are killed. We will kill them and they will kill us. But remember we are different from them.

Through this pep talk, the young fighters were given a dose of Boko Haram's ideology. Boko Haram commanders do not shy away from the fact that it is quite likely that in battle some of their young fighters would die – this is clearly stated – but the important point is that the commanders explain that these young men are to be distinguished from the enemy because, even though some of them will die, they will have access to salvation and paradise. The extent to which such talks bolstered young men is unclear, and a number of the foot soldiers on camera look nervous – but it is an indication that, at least for the leadership level of the movement, ideology was still an important factor. In an interview (VOA 2017b) with one former Boko Haram member ("Donaldi"), not a part of Boko Haram's own footage, it was recounted that:

> If you refuse to carry a gun, Boko Haram will tell you to lie down. They will cut off your head and will put it on the back of your dead body or chest. And in some cases, they even cut open the chest and took the hearts out. That's how they frightened us into carrying a gun.

While this was not shown on Boko Haram's footage, it is an important point as it demonstrates Boko Haram's willingness to take brutal measures to compel young men to fight for their cause. The young men in Boko Haram's video are shown attacking a garrison in the town of Banki. The garrison was guarded with tanks, and after struggling to get their anti-aircraft guns (mounted on the back of pickup trucks) to work, and with casualties mounting, Boko Haram withdrew. It is interesting that such footage of failure was retained, though it does serve to show that the footage was not intended for propaganda purposes, but rather for internal use, and as such makes it more candid as to what was going on in 2015.

Given the bleak conditions under Boko Haram in northeastern Nigeria, it was jarring to see footage of young Boko Haram foot soldiers enjoying downtime in their camps when not engaged in more violent activities. These young men are shown laughing and enjoying themselves and, like most teenagers anywhere, challenging each other to various types of competitions. In one segment, young men are shown doing cartwheels and handstands, while in other segments they are engaged in push-up competitions while other members of the movement watch and cheer. The young men are also shown breakdancing, racing by hopping on one leg, and riding on motorbikes, as well as singing Islamic hymns together. It is likely that such activities tighten the bonds of brotherhood between Boko Haram members and are also a way to maintain cohesion within the group (Hegghammer 2017). Now that Boko Haram has lost the majority of its territory, it is my hope that testimonies can be gathered from those affected by the violence of the movement, and in time, where possible, from those who participated in that violence, to give a more complete picture of what Boko Haram's Islamist rule looked like.

The call for *shari'a*

This chapter has argued that Boko Haram managed to achieve, albeit for a short period of time, one of its longstanding goals – the carving out of territory in northeastern Nigeria in which Islamic law was implemented. This desire has to be situated in the broader context of the calls for the implementation of Islamic law in Nigeria, as well as the judicial history of the country. Islam, as discussed in Chapter Two, has been widespread in northern Nigeria for centuries, with the population predominantly Muslim. Precolonial governments in the region applied *shari'a* law in various degrees and certainly regarded themselves as legitimate Islamic entities. Under British colonialism, the colonial government (c. 1914–1960) allowed *shari'a* courts to implement *shari'a* law in civil cases, but this was not extended to criminal matters. By 1958, towards the end of colonial rule in Nigeria, the northern regional government sought the advice of a panel which included the Chief Justice of Sudan, a judge of the supreme court of Pakistan, one British expert of Islamic law, and three Nigerians to reform the penal law and courts. Addressing the then House of Chiefs, Ahmed Bello, the premier of the region said:

There is nothing in the central recommendation of the Panel that a new Penal Code of criminal law should be introduced into the region that is in any way contrary to the tenets of our religion. The new code will be almost identical with those which have been in force for years in the Sudan and Pakistan and which have been proved perfectly acceptable to the millions of Moslems among the populations of those countries.

(Bello 1962: 217–218)

The judicial situation of northern Nigeria remained stable for the period of the northern regional government's administration (1960–1966), as well as in the period of the military interregnum, without drawing significant public debate. It was from 1977 to 1979, when civilian rule was to resume in Nigeria, that the position of *shari'a* law in the Nigerian constitution generated heated debate. What emerged from those debates was a middle-ground position in the form of Section 275 of the Constitution of the Federal Republic of Nigeria, 1999, namely that there would be no Federal *Shari'a* Court of Appeal, but 'there shall be for any state that requires it, a *Shari'a* Court of Appeal for that state.' For some, the passions ignited over the debates surrounding *Shari'a* law opened up an opportunity to further politicize the issue, and this was to happen following the 1999 Nigerian transition to democracy. Sani Ahmed Yerima, the governor of Zamfara state in northwestern Nigeria, pledged in March 2000 to expand the scope of the jurisdiction of *shari'a* courts to include criminal cases. Yerima, described as a 'former henchman of General Babangida, refashioned himself as a proponent of Islamic law for self-serving reasons and subsequently pushed for full *shari'a* across the state' (Varin 2016: 47). Yerima's expansion of *shari'a* law drew widespread attention, and Muslim communities in the north responded with enthusiasm. Crowds

appeared at rallies across the north to pressure state governors . . . to adopt Yerima's course, or to welcome new states into the *shari'a* fold. Following Yerima's announcement, bus and taxi drivers reduced fares into Zamfara in a show of solidarity.

(Kendhammer 2013: 294)

Eleven other states in northern Nigeria followed suit in expanding the scope of *shari'a* law, and these states enacted written laws and punishments prescribed for consumption of alcohol, prostitution, and theft, among many other "sins." The move to reinstating *shari'a* cannot be seen as purely an Islamist drive in the north, but rather a move that also carried much popular support, with the Qadriyya and Tijaniyya Sufi brotherhoods often at the forefront (Pieri et al. 2014). The drive for the expansion of *shari'a* law was popular among Muslims in northern Nigeria because of a strong perception that it was an antidote to corruption. In common with Muslims in other parts of the world during this time, society was viewed to be in a state of moral decline, with Islamic values being destroyed by western cultural hegemony, an argument that Boko Haram was also able to capitalize upon in their early drives for recruitment. As one interviewee put it, the argument used by Boko Haram was that

> *shari'a* was the only option left. Nigeria tried everything else from dictatorship to democracy, capitalism to cronyism, and nothing worked. The only solution to corruption, immorality, and the sorry state of affairs in the north was *shari'a* and that is because *shari'a* is incorruptible; it is not decided by man, but dictated by Allah.

Such arguments were powerful and were by no means limited to Boko Haram, but rather were part of the mainstream dialogue at the time and found resonance among the Muslim population.

As pressure mounted for the further Islamization of society, by 2003 the northern state of Kano introduced a societal re-orientation program which targeted rural and urban communities, the private and public sectors, women, and youths (The Economist 2007). This program identified more than a hundred sins to be combated and listed moral values to be instilled. Sins were wide ranging and included apathy, poor personal health care, idleness, early marriages, and family abandonment. "Urban sins" included individualism, elitism, child trafficking, political brigandage, and sale and reading of licentious books. Kano, as with some other northern Nigerian states, went further to establish a *hisbah* board with thousands of uniformed personnel to implement the social reorientation program and to police sin in public places. According to Saidu Ahmad Dukawa, director general of Kano's *hisbah*, 'The role of the *hisbah* is to command people to do what is good and prevent what is evil . . . we have seen an increase in good morals since we started, such as a fall in prostitution and more women voluntarily wearing the hijab' (The Economist 2010). The duties of the *hisbah* included checking that market traders do not swindle customers and tracking down brothels. In reality, however, the most profound impacts were felt in more common areas of life, for example in the inability to consume alcohol, listen to music, smoke cigarettes, or engage in gambling. There were also moral aspects that specifically impacted women, and these included the promotion of veiling for women as well as the strict segregation of the genders, which often meant that women were limited in their freedoms to travel and interact with others outside of their homes.

The *shari'a*-implementing states enacted laws prohibiting the sale and consumption of alcohol in public, or even in private, and *hisbah* patrols were empowered to confiscate beer. While no specific laws were created

against the use of non-religious music, the state censorship boards moni-
tored the lyrics of songs as well as clothing and dancing in music videos.
The concern of the *hisbah* in particular was that the use of disrespectful
language and clothing, seen as part of western culture, has the ability to
corrupt Islamic culture. In an interview, Bala Mohammed, Director General
of the Kano State Directorate for Societal Reorientation, commented that
(Mejia-Johnson & Piracha 2012),

> We are particular about rap, we are particular on film making, these are
> areas which we think would damage the culture if allowed to prolifer-
> ate. We don't want the language of rap. If you want to do rap music
> in Hausa [language] you have to throw away the swear words, you
> have to throw away the baggy trousers, you have to throw away insults
> to elders and others, you have to throw away the drug culture – the
> Islamic culture cannot take that.

From the northern Nigerian perspective, globalization propelled these
"sins," pushing them as part of a western cultural hegemony that would
erode Islamic values and corrupt Muslims from their faith. The implementation of *shari'a* and creation of *hisbah* patrols was a way of obliterating
sin in the public space and providing an antidote to what was seen as moral
decline and an erosion of traditional Muslim culture in the north. While
the move towards *shari'a* may be rooted in popular origins, there is also
an understanding now that the *hisbah* may have gone further than initially
expected, especially concerning the policing of the mixing of genders and
dress codes. The use of *hisbah* police caused a row between the state and the
federal government that ended up before the judiciary. Consequently, the
hisbah does not have much clout under Nigerian federal law. The officers
are not allowed to make arrests; they can only preach at miscreants or alert
the federal police, who often refuse to cooperate (The Economist 2010).

In the face of dwindling hope in the federal state structure, Hausaland
dug deep into its history and collective memory to find an identity that
would ground its passion for change. This identity was "Islam." The power
of "Islam" as a proper noun is powerfully buttressed in Hausaland by the
memory, now legendary for many, of the Sokoto Caliphate, which marked
one of the most important periods of rule in African modernity. "Islam" in
this construction carries the symbolic value of strength and perseverance, a
sense that all – rich or poor – are equal before God (Eltanatawi 2017: 17).
Idealized *shari'a* is what was demanded on the streets of northern Nigeria
in 1999; it was a constructed *shari'a* imbued with what Nigerians most
urgently want to see in their societies – an end to poverty and corruption.
An end to poverty and corruption thus became synonymous with idealized

shari'a. Political *shari'a* is what happened when *shari'a* took hold in the same corrupt political process that had prompted the revolution to begin with. While the ideal persists, the political manifestation of the ideal brings grief – and, in the age of Boko Haram, grave dangers for ordinary Nigerians (Eltantawi 2017: 14–15).

Notes

1 Shekau, A. 2014. 'Declaration of an Islamic Caliphate', in Kassim A. and Nwankpa, M. (eds.). *The Boko Haram Reader: From Nigerian Preachers to the Islamic State*. Oxford: Oxford University Press, pp. 321–326.
2 Shekau, A. 2015. 'Bay'a (Oath of Allegiance) to the Caliph of the Muslims', in Kassim A. and Nwankpa, M. (eds.). *The Boko Haram Reader: From Nigerian Preachers to the Islamic State*. Oxford: Oxford University Press, pp. 407–410.
3 A United Nations report (OCHA 2017) on September 30, 2017, showed that eastern Yobe State, northeastern Adamawa State, and virtually all of Borno State, aside from its capital of Maiduguri and other large towns, remain 'not accessible' or 'partially accessible' because of the 'threat of insurgent attacks.'
4 Formation of Jama'at Ansar al-Muslimin Fi Bilad al-Sudan, in Kassim, A. and Nwankpa, M. 2018. *The Boko Haram Reader: From Nigerian Preachers to the Islamic State*. Oxford: Oxford University Press, pp. 253–256.
5 Shekau, A. 2015. 'Bay'a to the Caliph of the Muslims', in Kassim, A. and Nwankpa, M. (eds.). *The Boko Haram Reader: From Nigerian Preachers to the Islamic State*. Oxford: Oxford University Press, pp. 407–410.
6 Nur, M. 2016. 'Expose: An Open Letter to Abubakar Shekau', in Kassim, A. and Nwankpa, M. (eds.). *The Boko Haram Reader: From Nigerian Preachers to the Islamic State*. Oxford: Oxford University Press, pp. 445–466.
7 Shekau, A. 2014. 'Declaration of an Islamic Caliphate', in Kassim A. and Nwankpa, M. (eds.). *The Boko Haram Reader: From Nigerian Preachers to the Islamic State*. Oxford: Oxford University Press, pp. 321–326.
8 Participant Interview, Osaro Odemwingie, April 25, 2015. Tampa, FL.
9 The footage is available on VOA's YouTube site, and may be accessed with the following link. www.youtube.com/playlist?list=PLMWxa-uE499GOnV8ky16 IDGnS2iGvDGpr (accessed: December 27, 2018).
10 Nur, M. 2009. 'Returning to the Quran and Sunna', in Kassim A. and Nwankpa, M. (eds.). *The Boko Haram Reader: From Nigerian Preachers to the Islamic State*. Oxford: Oxford University Press, pp. 151–159.

6   Beyond Boko Haram?

Introduction

On August 21, 2018, Mamman Nur, a longtime Boko Haram commander, mastermind 'behind the ties between Boko Haram and Abu Bakr al-Baghdadi's led Islamic State,' and a senior leader of the Islamic State West Africa Province (ISWAP) faction, was killed. His death did not come as part of a Nigerian security services operation, nor as part of any military effort against the movement, but rather at the hands of his own followers who 'rebelled against him' (Sahara Reporters 2018a). Nur, often described as the brains of Boko Haram, was killed by his 'closest lieutenants, for releasing the Dapchi girls,[1] without demanding ransom, among other reasons' (Sahara Reporters 2018b). His death is a forewarning that Boko Haram, known for its brutal tactics such as suicide bombings, the kidnapping and sexual enslavement of women, and the killing of those that oppose its ideologies, is becoming even more extreme. Despite his repeated calls for jihad in west Africa, and the desire to see the establishment of an Islamic state mirroring that of Usman dan Fodio's and linked to the caliphal claims of Baghdadi's Islamic State, Nur was 'slightly more moderate than the longtime leader of Boko Haram, Abubakar Shekau who rejoices in enslaving girls and "killing anyone God commands me to kill"' (The Economist 2018). Nur, by contrast, sought to mitigate some of Shekau's more extremist tactics through arguing that the movement should 'only attack military targets, and that using children as human bombs might not be an act of unblemished piety' (The Economist 2018). Nur had theological disagreements with Shekau, especially over *takfir*. Shekau's steadfastness in applying this concept to all those that disagreed with him ultimately led to the fracturing of Boko Haram. The first split occurred with the emergence of Ansaru in 2011, and while Ansaru reintegrated with Boko Haram in 2013, the ideological differences between the two remained, resurfacing in 2016 and ultimately leading to the removal of Shekau by the Islamic State as the emir of ISWAP. The killing of Nur by his own followers highlights the fractious inner workings of Boko Haram. This episode allows for a focus on the reasons that lead to splits within the movement, and provides insight as to the possible future evolution of its tactics and strategy.

This chapter discusses the concept of *takfir*, explaining how it came to form an important part of Shekau's justifications for killing opponents. It will be argued that battles over the interpretation and application of *takfir* acted not only as a driver of Boko Haram's violence but also as a double edged-sword, causing the movement to split and, in part, to further radicalize. The chapter will demonstrate how the use and misuse of *takfir* was instrumental in fracturing Boko Haram, with special attention to the removal of Abubakar Shekau as the emir of ISWAP. The consequence of this was to create two distinct and competing factions of Boko Haram – one allied to Baghdadi's Islamic State and led by Abu Musab al-Barnawi (a son of Boko Haram's former leader, Mohammad Yusuf), and another led by Abubakar Shekau. Shekau's faction is widely seen as more willing to use indiscriminate tactics of violence to gain its objectives and has a far looser application of *takfir* than the more orthodox, yet still exceptionally violent, ISWAP faction. Shekau's faction has also been more willing to operationalize the abduction of women and their use in suicide terrorism, causing further friction among the factions (Nnam et al. 2018: 37).

Through focusing on its key leaders and ideologies, the chapter will outline Boko Haram's evolution with regards to its stance on *takfirism* and argue that the ways in which *takfir* has been interpreted have acted as a driver of the most brutal forms of Boko Haram's violence. This battle over the interpretation of *takfir* is still active today. With the declining influence of the Islamic State among jihadist movements and the killing of Mamman Nur, the potential is there for Shekau's unrestrained application of the concept to emerge supreme. This would have a devastating effect on the civilian population and, at the same time, continue to alienate Boko Haram from those whom it claims to be fighting for.

Takfir

The concept of and application of *takfir*, though deeply controversial in Islam, has become a powerful tool in the theological arsenal of jihadist movements, not least for Boko Haram. *Takfir* is a religious concept which allows the act of excommunication – declaring a nominal Muslim an infidel or apostate (*kufr*) (Akhlaq 2015: 1). This is significant because the prescribed punishment in Islam for those deemed to be apostates is death. As such the declaration of *takfir* by jihadist movements on those Muslims who disagree with their ideology has become a convenient way dispose of their "enemies." Traditionally, declaring *takfir* upon a Muslim was no easy task, was treated with the utmost severity, and could 'only be pronounced by qualified religious authorities under very specific circumstances' (Hegghammer 2009: 247).

The Qur'an stipulates that Muslims should not excommunicate other Muslims who consider themselves Muslim, even if some of their practices do not always outwardly conform to Islam (Qur'an 4:94). This directive is also found in the *hadith*; for example, Ibn Umar reported the prophet Mohammad as saying that, 'When a man calls his brother an unbeliever, it returns at least to one of them.'[2] Even so, after the death of Mohammad, the issue of *takfir* grew, threatening to tear apart the Muslim community, and climaxed after the assassination of Islam's third caliph, Uthman, in 656. Ali ibn Talib, the cousin and son-in-law of the prophet Mohammad who became Islam's fourth caliph, faced strong opposition from Mu'awiya ibn Abu Sufyan, one of Uthman's close relatives and the governor of Damascus. Mu'awiya accused Ali of 'harboring Uthman's assassins and demanded extradition so that he could fulfil his vendetta, according to tribal customs' (Wiktorowicz 2006: 228). The two armies engaged in battle at Siffin in 657 and later agreed to submit to arbitration by two referees who would settle the dispute according to the Qur'an. A number of fighters from Ali's side felt 'betrayed by his decision to submit to human arbitration and turned against him. The Khawarij, as they became known, argued that, "God alone has the right to judge" and declared Ali an apostate' (Wiktorowicz 2006: 228).

The Kharijites were the first identifiable group in Islamic history to be concerned with the issue of *takfir* and with defining the extent to which one could deviate from Islamic norms and still be considered Muslim (Zenn & Pieri 2017: 288). The Kharijite position was that 'Muslims who commit grave sins effectively reject their religion, entering the ranks of apostates, and therefore deserve capital punishment' (Sonn & Farrar 2009). The majority of Muslims rejected this position as extreme, threatening the cohesiveness of the community. As Brigaglia (2018: 201–202) notes, the term 'kharijite' is today 'loosely applied by Muslims to any group that allegedly manifest extremism or rejects "legitimate" authority' and as such 'mainstream Sunnis often use the label for Salafis as a whole; mainstream Salafis apply it to the jihadis; and jihadis like al Qaeda and the Islamic State apply it to Boko Haram's leader Shekau.'

Takfir continued to remain controversial even amongst the most orthodox of Islamist groups, though several Islamists have attempted to reinterpret and apply the concept to contemporary times. The most famous of these was Sayyid Qutb, who used *takfir* to provide a 'legal loophole around the prohibition of killing other Muslims, and made it a religious obligation to execute the apostate' (Zenn & Pieri 2017: 288). The obvious use of this concept was to declare secular rulers, officials or organizations, or any Muslims that opposed the Islamist agenda a *kafir* [infidel] thereby justifying assassinating them (Eikmeier 2007: 89). It is this kind of interpretation of *takfir* that has been demonstrated by Shekau in both discourse and actions. This was prominent in a speech from January 2015, in which Shekau warned Muslims in Cameroon that the only way they would be considered true Muslims and saved from attack was by abandoning any ties to democratic practice:

> O people of Cameroon, you should know that a person does not become a Muslim except by disassociation from democracy and all other polytheistic acts. It is obligatory upon you to disbelieve and disassociate yourself from democracy. It is also obligatory upon you to declare disassociation from democracy's servants and helpers.[3]

This shows that for Shekau, even if Muslims outwardly express Islamic practices such as keeping to the pillars of Islam, they should still be considered as unbelievers if they engage in democracy.

Attempts at the application of *takfir* by contemporary jihadist groups such as Boko Haram have had brutal consequences for many Muslim civilians who refuse to recognize the legitimacy of those jihadist movements. Since its inception, Boko Haram leaders have repudiated the legitimacy of the Nigerian state and chosen to withdraw from what they regarded as a morally corrupt society around them (Serano & Pieri 2014: 199). It was not until Shekau became leader that Boko Haram started pronouncing *takfir*. Shekau's liberal use of *takfir* led to growing opposition to him and caused a fissure between Boko Haram and Islamic State, and it is this point of contention that the remainder of the chapter will analyze.

Shekau, *takfir*, and the first splits in Boko Haram

Abubakar Shekau has been the face of Boko Haram since taking the helm of the movement's leadership after Mohammad Yusuf's extrajudicial killing. Despite appearing in numerous videos taunting the Nigerian government and rejoicing at the brutality of Boko Haram's tactics, little is known about him. One source that does shed light on Shekau's background and character is *Slicing the Tumor* (ISWAP 2018). Though this tract is biased against Shekau with the intention of establishing him as a modern-day Khajirite, there are some important details that add much to his background. He is described as having had a 'harsh upbringing,' in which 'he did not know the colors of luxury or the phenomena of wealth,' and that as a boy he served 'under farmers to support himself with money' (ISWAP 2018). Shekau started his education 'in the circles of the 'ulama of al-Zawaya until he memorized the Qur'an among them' and then moved to Maiduguri where he enrolled at the High Islam Institute, though abandoning his studies there when realizing its links to Sufism, and instead reorienting to a Salafist version of Islam (ISWAP 2018). It was with this reorientation, according to the authors of *Slicing the Tumor* (2018), that Shekau started to join Mohammad Yusuf's activities, becoming his closest disciple, noted for his piety and austerity:

> I remember that he had a motorbike on which he ate the handles and drank [meaning it had become very old], so some of the charitable brothers wanted to buy him a different one, which he totally rejected. And he was not convinced until they insisted on him to replace it, and if he were given new clothes he would not accept them or he would donate them if he received them.

The Shekau presented here is a man of seemingly deep piety and moral authority – living the message that Yusuf was preaching at the time about the importance of a distinct community of Muslims marked out by their sincerity and allegiance to *shari'a* law. Shekau is further credited as having held Boko Haram together following Yusuf's killing, for having inspired the movement's followers to take up arms in a call to jihad, and for facilitating contacts with AQIM. It is at this point that the narrative starts to turn against Shekau, who it is argued started to show 'signs of extremism,' which included (ISWAP 2018):

> Denying the excuse in ignorance in *kufr* [infidels] absolutely, and *takfiring* [apostizing] the Muslims dwelling in the land of *kufr* [infidels] as individuals, deeming their blood and wealth not to be sacrosanct for protection, and the group's method in conveying the *da'wa* [proselytization] and dealing with the masses changed fundamentally, and Shekau treated those in the group close to him with tyranny and unfairness.

Evidenced is that Shekau embarked on a path of taking it upon himself to define who could be considered as a "true" Muslim, and because of this, there were profound implications for Boko Haram's ideological and tactical evolution, as well as with its relationship to the wider population of northern Nigeria. As per the example above, Shekau argued that Muslims living in areas that were not deemed to be Muslim no longer qualified as Muslims and so could be looted and/or killed. This form of *takfir* being developed and implemented by Shekau not only caused consternation among members of Boko Haram but also sparked a letter of advice from AQIM, which it is claimed Shekau ignored (ISWAP 2018).

Because of the deep disagreements around the definition and application of *takfir*, a number of rifts emerged in Boko Haram. The authors of *Slicing the Tumor* note that Shekau was able to maintain the upper hand because the 'vast majority of the *mujahideen* stood confused,' and Shekau 'ordered the commanders to prevent the soldiers from listening to any of the contrarians, and he kept away from them messages and statements except what came out from him' (ISWAP 2018). For this reason, 'there was no message except what came from Shekau' while at the same time Shekau 'slandered' his opponents in his 'statements and rebuffed them. He also killed some of them, which made the group be flooded in a sea of ignorance and transgression' (ISWAP 2018). This is why Ansaru split from Boko Haram, causing the first major fissure in the movement.

Ansaru, whose core leaders included Mamman Nur and Khalid al-Barnawi, was aligned to AQIM and had actively sought al Qaeda's support in tempering Shekau's stance on *takfir*. This point was reinforced in a string of letters, released by AQIM in April 2017, highlighting discussions between Boko Haram and AQIM from before 2011 and including complaints to AQIM about Shekau (Oriola & Akinola 2018: 602–603). The letter, signed by Khalid al-Barnawi and his consultative council (*shura*) says, 'Shekau spends his time proclaiming *takfir*,' and 'all of this has led the Nigerian people to criticize the religion and jihad, causing general chaos,' and that Shekau uses '*takfir* for all who participate in elections disregarding the principles and rules of *takfir*' (Rashid 2017). In addition, the letters argue that Shekau's theological reference points for understanding *takfir* are deviant, and they compare Shekau to the Armed Islamic Group (GIA), from which AQIM's predecessor, the Salafist Group for Preaching and Combat (known by its French acronym GSPC), split during the Algerian civil war in the 1990s because of the GIA's excessive *takfir* (Zenn & Pieri 2017: 296).

One of the fundamental impacts of the splitting of Boko Haram in 2011 was to entrench the doctrine of *takfir* into the official ideology and tactics of the movement. Because most of those with a scholarly background in Islamic theology and texts vacated the movement, any form of check on how Shekau was interpreting or implementing *takfir* was removed. This provided 'fertile grounds for the emergence of all sorts of extremism' by Boko Haram's lay members, including 'highway robberies directed at the Muslim commoners, whose loot was considered as legitimate booty of war based on Shekau's blanket excommunication of the Muslim masses' (Brigaglia 2018: 212).

Boko Haram and Islamic State

The rise of Baghdadi's Islamic State, with its declaration of a new Islamic caliphate, the quick and vast acquisition of territories in Iraq and Syria, and the mass recruitment of jihadists from all over the world, including Muslims in western Europe and North America, was to make a dramatic impact on the international jihadist scene (McCants 2015). Seen as a new epicenter of power and moral authority for jihadist movements, many started to court the Islamic State, seeking partnerships and in some cases a desire for being named as an official franchise of the Islamic State. Boko Haram, despite the ties of some of its commanders to al Qaeda, was an early aspirant to forming an alliance with the Islamic State, a move which was solidified in 2015 and which was to have a bearing on the ideological and tactical evolution of the movement, not to mention its renaming as ISWAP. The merger between Boko Haram and the Islamic State must be seen in the context of the reintegration of Ansaru into Boko Haram (see Chapter 5), and which for the first time in the history of the insurgency led to Boko Haram carving out territory in northeastern Nigeria in 2014. With Boko Haram seemingly on the up (though in actuality starting to incur losses), in March 2015, Shekau pledged allegiance to the Islamic State, which was recognized by the Islamic State (Bryson & Bukarti 2018).

The internal dynamics of the pledge of allegiance from Boko Haram to the Islamic State were not as straightforward as they might first seem and indeed were driven by the same dynamics that had previously split Boko Haram. It emerged that while Shekau had initiated the oath of allegiance to Baghdadi, the true impetus for this came from former Ansaru members such as Mamman Nur and Abu Fatima. Nur argued that it was 'obligatory to pledge allegiance to the Caliph once he appears in the world' and claimed that Shekau feared that, by not pledging allegiance to Baghdadi, Abu Musab al-Barnawi, Mamman Nur, and Abu Fatima would have formed a breakaway faction, declaring their own allegiance and thus taking the momentum away from Shekau (Zenn & Pieri 2017: 298). These senior commanders saw the emergence of the Islamic State and its newfound influence over the international jihadist scene as 'an occasion to moderate the extremism of the Nigerian jihadi autocrat [Shekau]' (Brigaglia 2018: 214). It is probable that Shekau may not have wanted to formally join the Islamic State and become an official franchise, instead preferring to initiate a looser form of mutual recognition and cooperation so as to not have to sacrifice his authority over Boko Haram. Indeed, this point was made rather clearly by the authors of *Slicing the Tumor*, who noted that Shekau was

> compelled to give allegiance, and that was through a coming together of the military commanders, and after he became convinced that the matter was about to go out of his hand, and that his throne would be shaken and emptied of him if he did not give allegiance, he gave allegiance to remain on his throne.
>
> (ISWAP 2018)

In the absence of evident operational links between the Islamic State and Boko Haram, the most concrete relationship was their social media coordination, including the Islamic State's setting up of a social media platform for Boko Haram in January 2015 showing videos, tweets, and statements (Zenn & Pieri 2017: 298). While this activity was visible on social media, behind-the- scenes it was Nigerian youths in Borno State who were doing most of the work. The Islamic State

> would send these youths, presumably by e-mail, the templates for videos and Islamic State *nasheeds* [hymns], and the youths would film Boko Haram attacks locally and incorporate the local footage with the Islamic State templates and then send them to the Islamic State, again presumably by e-mail, for the Islamic State to disseminate on its social media channels.
>
> (Pieri & Zenn 2018: 666)

It is through an analysis of the media content of Boko Haram during the 2015–2016 period that questions emerged about the role that Shekau was playing in leading Boko Haram under the Islamic State's tutelage.

The role of Shekau's leadership *vis-à-vis* the Islamic State was first raised at the end of January 2015, when a video emerged in which Abu Musab al-Barnawi (one of Mohammad Yusuf's sons and later an ISWAP leader) was interviewed regarding Boko Haram attacks on the town of Baga which had occurred earlier that month. Boko Haram fighters entered Baga on January 3, 2015, on foot and on motorbikes, 'indiscriminately shooting at unarmed civilians' whose dead 'bodies . . . littered the streets' and continued to massacre civilians in Baga and the surrounding villages until January 7, 2015 (Muscati & Hassan 2015). According to Human Rights Watch (2015), Baga may have been the deadliest single massacre in the Boko Haram conflict, with estimates of up to 2,000 people killed, homes burned to the ground, and hundreds of people abducted. The video dating from January 27 was unique as it was issued 'under a new media agency, *al-'Urwa al-Wuthqa*, and did not mention Shekau at all, while the style and contents of the videos carry many of the messages of Ansaru, protesting Muslim civilian deaths' (Kassim & Nwankpa 2018: 369). It was this non-mention of Shekau that stood out as important, signaling that fractures within the movement were still in place and that, perhaps, al-Barnawi had managed to bypass Shekau in putting out his own interpretation of what happened in Baga. The message from al-Barnawi's camp was that 'we are not killing innocent civilians. Our mission is to return to return the law of Allah on the earth and to reform the empire of Usman dan Fodio, which was conquered by the colonists.'[4] The fact remained that Shekau had authorized the indiscriminate killing of

Muslims through his own vision of *takfir*, and as such came to be viewed as a problem by the more orthodox minded Boko Haram commanders, as well as by the Islamic State's leadership. Because of this, there was a marked absence of Shekau in propaganda material (especially from March 2015 to September 2015, and from September 2015 to March 2016) from Boko Haram and a distinctly more theological nature to the content.

As well as the issue of *takfir*, there was growing concern among some more orthodox-minded Boko Haram commanders over Shekau's excessive use of female suicide bombers in Boko Haram's campaigns against the Nigerian government and people. According to Warner and Matfess (2017: v), Boko Haram, which first used a male bomber in 2011, had by 2017 become dependent on females:

> Boko Haram has deployed not only more total female bombers than any other terrorist group in history, but more female suicide bombers as a percentage of its overall suicide bombing cadre than any other group . . . Female bombers tend to focus on different targets than men. Whereas men tend to target mostly Christian and governmental institutions, women are far more prone to target civilian locations.

The first recorded female suicide bombing took place in June 2014, in the northeastern state of Gombe, and has since been followed by female suicide bombers blowing themselves up in crowded marketplaces, college campuses, banks, mosques, and other public spaces (Nnam et al. 2018: 37–38). Data shows that Boko Haram deployed 469 female suicide bombers in 240 total incidents from June 2014 to the end of February 2018, killing an estimated 1,259 people (1,673 people with bombers included) and injuring 2,967 more people (Pearson 2018: 34).

The strategic deployment of women as bombers 'entails the power to decide whether or not a woman's body becomes an instrument of death, which suicide bombing encodes in both physical and symbolic senses' (Pereira 2018: 255). The (mis)use of women and girls in such ways by Boko Haram continues to highlight the movement's capacity to 'outdo the security services in inflicting brutality and repression while eluding their own capture,' as well as 'constituting yet another graphic display . . . of the insurgents' continued power to disrupt everyday life, even in the face of territorial losses' (Pereira 2018: 255).

Due to Shekau's heavy reliance on female suicide bombers, his faction may have contravened the established norms of martyrdom as put forward by the Islamic State, as well as 'the majority view of Salafi-jihadi scholars that women should neither fight nor engage in suicide bombings' (Pearson 2018: 34). Yet, as Pearson (2018: 34) notes, Islamic State leadership appears to have tacitly endorsed Shekau's use of female suicide terrorism, and rather than 'criticize Boko Haram for challenging its gendered ideology, the Islamic State instead emphasized high-profile actions that apparently cohered with it, such as the abduction and "sale" of the Chibok schoolgirls, which was praised in *Dabiq* Issue 8 *"Shari'a* Alone Will Rule Africa."' Having said this, it also appears that the issue of gender-based violence played a part in the factional struggles within Boko Haram, with al-Barnawi reportedly disapproving 'of Shekau's use of girl children as bombers,' with the issue emerging as a 'source of tension between Boko Haram leaders that eventually led to splits' (Pearson 2018: 41).

Islamic State and the fracturing of Boko Haram

On August 2, 2016, Abubakar Shekau was removed ISWAP's emir. The news first broke in Islamic State's *al-Naba* newsletter (number 41), in which Abu Musab al-Barnawi, previously known as a Boko Haram spokesman, was interviewed as ISWAP's newly appointed governor. In essence this meant that Shekau had been removed from this position, which he had held since pledging allegiance to the Islamic State in March 2015. In this newsletter, al-Barnawi made it clear that the mission of the movement was 'against Christianizing activities in Africa, and answered some of the suspicions raised by Islamic scholars regarding Boko Haram' (Kassim & Nwankpa 2018: 441). On August 3, 2018, a ten-minute audio was released by Shekau, angry at his demotion from ISWAP's governorship. The contents of this audio message provide important details explaining Shekau's demotion, as well as some of the behind-the-scenes wrangling by Boko Haram members and the Islamic State over *takfir*. The announcement of Abu Musab al-Barnawi as ISAWP's new governor gave an early indication that the Islamic State was not supportive of Shekau's interpretation of *takfir* and instead wanted a more constrained interpretation and implementation, fearing that otherwise any goodwill among the Muslim population that such movements often count upon would be completely lost. The central dispute around the issue of *takfir* was captured in Shekau's audio message[5]:

> My brothers in Allah, I received a message you sent regarding the selection of a new Governor. My brothers, Abu Musab al-Barnawi and those with him are saying that if a Muslim enters a land of unbelief, but does not manifest his enmity to the unbelievers there, he is not an unbeliever. However, we say that such a person is an unbeliever. Afterwards, they said that if he [a Muslim] does not show his enmity to the *taghut* [illegitimate ruler] who rules by [something] other than Allah's revealed

law, he is not an unbeliever. However, we say that such a person is an unbeliever . . . As a result, we cannot follow a person who commits a major [act of] unbelief or polytheism, knowingly, with an explanation, and not based on misinterpretation. No, this is not possible. You do not know the condition of this group, yet we have sent you many letters, eight letters [in total], to show us the truth of this matter in the Book and the Sunna. However, you did not say anything [in response] nor did you answer, except for us to hear this news [of substituting Shekau as governor for al-Barnawi].

It is evident then, that the concept of *takfir* – its interpretation and imple-mentation – were central to the internal discussions and disputes that were occurring within Boko Haram. It is also clear that al-Baghdadi and the wider leadership of the Islamic State were aware of this issue and that a level of correspondence had been exchanged on the matter until al-Baghdadi had stopped responding to Shekau, instead replacing him with Abu Musab al-Barnawi.

Between the summer of 2015 and the spring of 2016, 'Boko Haram car-ried out a long string of suicide attacks, usually using young female suicide attackers, against mosques, market places, and refugee centers' throughout northeastern Nigeria and northern Cameroon (Kassim & Nwankpa 2018: 445; Olaniyan 2017). It is likely that Shekau was punishing Boko Har-am's former subjects for now being back under the control of the Nigerian government, something Shekau may have regarded as a state of apostasy (Kassim & Nwankpa 2018: 445). The constant level of brutality against the population, and in particular attacks against Muslims and mosques, sanctioned by the notion of *takfir* was seen as deeply egregious by senior commanders within Boko Haram as well as the leadership of the Islamic State. The justification for Shekau's removal as emir of ISWAP was to play out in a very public way as the two sides (Shekau and the Islamic State), released communiques arguing their cases and the evidence for how and why decisions were reached. The clearest allegations against Shekau come from an open letter released by Mamman Nur on August 4, 2016, in which he launched a scathing attack on Shekau and his leadership.[6] Nur outlines several reasons why Shekau had fallen into deep sin for his actions, includ-ing Shekau's insistence on interpreting *takfir*, fighting those who are not supposed to be fought, interpreting the Qur'an through his own framework, and killing those who have expressed opposition to him, among other items.

On the matter of *takfir*, Nur was clear, telling Shekau that 'the ruling on *takfir* should not be dictated by you, because Islam is not in your personal possession that you can admit or expel whoever you want.'[7] In essence Shekau was being accused of having deviated from the accepted norms of Qur'anic interpretation and was being reminded that it 'is only Allah who can dictate who is a Muslim and an unbeliever based upon evidence in the Book and Sunna.'[8] For Nur, Shekau's ideology was simply expressed as 'whoever is not with him are unbelievers and shedding their blood is permissible,' which Nur and other more orthodox-minded commanders of Boko Haram reject: 'we do not agree with such an interpretation and never have we understood Islam in that way. I hope it is understood.'[9] The issue of *takfir* is one that Nur labors throughout the letter, returning to the point several times, noting that 'you should not personalize Islam. You cannot order that someone be killed because that person insulted you. You cannot order that someone be killed because someone criticized you.'[10] The letter, while addressed to Shekau, is clearly aimed at a much broader audience – to other members of Boko Haram, to the leadership of the Islamic State, and perhaps even to wider Salafi-jihadist movements. This is because Nur was attempting to delegitimize Shekau through drawing upon accepted Salafist interpretations of *takfir* while reassuring a wider audience that the removal of Shekau was in accordance with Salafi principles and reasoning.

As well as the issue of *takfir*, Nur provided a character assassination of Shekau, presenting him as someone who is interested only in himself, without any concern for those beneath him – including foot soldiers of the movement, as well as those Boko Haram was ruling over. This is evident in the following accusation: 'you do not care. You left soldiers, students, and women in a state of hunger, thirst and agony. It is not as if there is no food. There is food but he refused to give it to them. We know he eats chicken. During the rainy season, twenty children died daily because of starvation.'[11] It is for these reasons, Nur explains, that:

> All of us here have rebelled from all those actions of yours. We are together with the caliphal state. We are not together with the unjust state, the state of killing, or the state that does whatever it wishes. We are together with the caliphal state. We are together with our leader Abubakar al-Baghdadi, the successor of Allah's messenger. We are together with him. Therefore if you say you will not follow him, you should know that you are the rebel. Before now, there were many actions taken by you where you refused to obey them. How many commands did they give you which you refused to follow? You are deceiving people. You even said that you regret pledging allegiance to them because you were compelled.[12]

While Nur provided clear reasons why he and other commanders in Boko Haram split from Shekau's faction, which reverted to the name of JAS after the split, and why the Islamic State removed Shekau as emir of ISWAP, there was also a series of rebuttals from Shekau and his followers. That such a dialogue was taking place in the form of open communiques allows for an unparalleled insight into the inner workings of the relationships between Boko Haram and the Islamic State. On August 7, 2016, a video was released by Shekau's faction expressing disdain at the demotion of Shekau as official emir of ISWAP, and Shekau's representative, Man Chari, argued that al-Barnawi was not a true Salafi and that he and other members of Boko Haram would continue to follow Shekau. The contents of the video, though released by Shekau's faction, are also rather embarrassing for Shekau, as it appears that Shekau was not formally told of his demotion; instead, 'the news was delivered to us through the unbeliever's media about the change to a new governor.'[13] It is also clear that Shekau wrote to Islamic State leadership on several occasions to discuss the ongoing concerns around the concept of *takfir*, but after the third letter, no further responses arrived. This at least shows that Shekau was interested enough in maintaining his position to write at length to the Islamic State. Man Chari noted that Shekau

> wrote to you eight letters in which he explained to you the ideology of *irja* [faith restricted to belief not deeds]. You asked him about the meaning of *irja*, and he explained to you in his third message but you did not respond. Before these issues we had already informed you that they split away from us, becoming isolated from us, but you did not do anything.[14]

This meant that Shekau was subordinate to Islamic State on certain organizational and theological matters. Shekau was also subordinate to Nur and al-Barnawi because Shekau had to operate through al-Barnawi to communicate with Islamic State and complained that al-Barnawi had been blocking his messages from getting to the Islamic State (Zenn 2018a: 17). In Shekau's part of the speech he reiterated that he was now the 'imam of JASDJ in west Africa,' formally signaling a split from ISWAP, though he did not renounce his allegiance to al-Baghdadi.

The dispute between ISWAP and JAS factions of Boko Haram were not resolved, as Shekau refused to accept that his interpretation of *takfir* was in error. On December 18, 2016, in an audio lecture, Shekau said that he would not be forced into believing 'that it is impossible for a Muslim to live in the unbelievers' land without the public manifestation of his religion, and still claim to be a Muslim.'[15] For Shekau, all Muslims have an obligation to wage jihad against secular and illegitimate leaders who fail to implement *shari'a* law as interpreted by Shekau, and that Muslims must purposefully migrate away from an area of "unbelief." Failure to do so, according to Shekau, constitutes an act of apostasy. In addition to this, Shekau reemphasized his opinion against the claim that 'it is impossible for a Muslim who has fought against an illegitimate ruler, who rules by means of constitution, to claim to be a Muslim or for him not to be labeled an unbeliever.'[16] Shekau states, regarding these types of scenarios:

> They wrote to us with the claim that they emanated from the caliphate [Islamic State]. They said I should agree and work with these creeds because that is how the caliphate is governed. Afterwards I said that these beliefs, if I did not hear them directly from the spokesman of the caliphate, I will not accept them. Whoever accepts these beliefs has committed apostasy. This is my creed.[17]

Beyond Boko Haram?

Due to the failure to reconcile over the different understandings of the interpretation and application of the concept of *takfir*, as well as the broader leadership style of Abubakar Shekau, two distinct factions of Boko Haram emerged which have at times have been in direct opposition to each other – both competing for a limited ranged of resources and recruits. The two branches are as follows: first, the Islamic State West Africa Province (ISWAP), led by Abu Musab al-Barnawi. It is part of the Islamic State, prioritizes loyalty to al-Baghdadi, and is more discriminating in its use of *takfir*. The second is *Jamaat Ahl as Sunnah Lid dawa wa al-Jihad* (JAS). This is a reversion to the original name of Boko Haram as established by Shekau in 2011. This branch is led by Shekau and is not affiliated with the Islamic State, despite Shekau not having formally rejected al-Baghdadi as caliph, and holds the most wide-reaching interpretation of *takfir*. It was this interpretation and application of *takfir* that divided Boko Haram and which spurred on some of the most brutal acts of violence in the history of the conflict.

The issue of *takfir* cannot be relegated to a mere theological dispute within the ranks of Boko Haram –rather, it is a central issue which eventually led to the Islamic State weighing in on the matter and Shekau's removal as emir of ISWAP. For Brigaglia (2018: 213), Shekau's combination of conceit and superficial knowledge of Islam were at the root of his most prolific 'doctrinal mistakes in the application of the rules of *takfir*.' Pointing to *Slicing the Tumor*, we are reminded that Shekau pronounced that 'any Muslim holding a Nigerian ID is an unbeliever' and advocated the position that 'who ever does not hold an unbeliever to be an unbeliever, or doubts about his status as an unbeliever, is an unbeliever himself' (Brigaglia 2018: 213). This extreme outlook on *takfir* had deep consequences, and between 2017 and 2018, after Boko Haram's division into ISWAP and JAS, the differences between the two crystalized.

One effect of this was the ultimate demise of Mamman Nur, who facilitated the return of the kidnapped Dapchi schoolgirls without taking any form of ransom payment (Aziken 2018). Despite the ISWAP faction having kidnapped 111 girls from their school in the town of Dapchi, the decision was taken to return these girls because the Islamic State demanded that only non-Muslims could be kidnapped or enslaved and that 'Muslim men and women, however, could not be enslaved; they could only be killed if they were apostates and did not repent' (Zenn 2018c). In Zenn's opinion, the schoolgirls, who were all Muslim (apart from one), may have been kidnapped by former Shekau loyalists who defected to al-Barnawi's faction and who may not have known about the prohibition against kidnapping Muslims. Once the girls were taken to Abu Musab's base near Lake Chad, al-Barnawi demanded their release, with the exception of the Christian girl, who under the Islamic State's rules was allowed to be enslaved (Zenn 2018c). According to a source quoted in the *Daily Trust*, a Nigerian newspaper, Nur was murdered because Boko Haram commanders 'became disenchanted with Nur's style of leadership,' whom they first agreed to support in revolt against Shekau 'because the argument back in 2014 was that Shekau was a hardliner who killed almost everyone, both Muslims and Christians who disagreed with his brand of Islam' (Idris & Sawab 2018). By 2018, however, many of these commanders may have felt that Nur, too, was compromising too much, and a major disagreement broke after the release of the Dapchi schoolgirls. According to the source (Idris & Sawab 2018), the negotiation of the release of the girls caused controversy amongst Boko Haram commanders:

> The negotiation of the release of the girls did not go down well with some close associates of Mamman Nur who released the girls unconditionally, following a directive by Al-Baghdadi. Nothing was paid before the girls were released and besides, Mamman Nur's soft approach and close contact to governments and different levels angered his foot soldiers who rebelled against him and thereafter executed him.

According to Major Salifu Bakari, a security expert quoted in the same *Daily Trust* article (Idris & Sawab 2018):

> The truth is Mamman Nur had lost control long before he was killed; the factional group was taken over by hardliners who share a lot in common with the Shekau faction whose landmarks include kidnapping, assault, abductions for ransom and other atrocities.

Given the losses that the Islamic State has incurred in Iraq and Syria, it is still unclear as to the level of influence the organization will exert over

Boko Haram in the future, or indeed, the impacts this might have on the jihadist scene in Africa. By the end of 2018, the Islamic State still held influence over the ISWAP faction of Boko Haram, as evidenced in continued ISWAP messaging on Islamic State social media channels. Indeed, according to Mahmood (2018), since August 23, 2018, attack claims from ISWAP have been promoted by Islamic State messaging outlets, which is of interest because

> only four similar attack claims were broadcast before July. Messaging shifts in the past have preceded major changes within the group, and the increased publicity of ISWP activities demonstrates at the least that virtual relations with Islamic State uninterrupted by Nur's reported demise.

ISWAP has also demonstrated an increase in attacks carried out on Nigerian military installations, with one example being the attack on a task force battalion in Metele which killed 118 soldiers, with another 150 missing (Ogundipe 2018). For Mahmood (2018), this indicates that ISWAP fighters have been able to 'loot weapons during raids,' and while no new territorial acquisitions have been made by the movement, 'the ability to dictate the pace of the war is a worrying sign of their capabilities in this part of Borno State.' This is something that was corroborated by Jacob Zenn, who visited Borno State in November 2018 and noted that 'more than anytime previously, ISWAP's decisions around attacks are closely reported through a chain-of-command to the leaders of IS, which is why the raids [of ISWAP] have resembled IS campaigns' (Zenn 2018b). What this means for the future direction of the Boko Haram factions and the ongoing conflict against Boko Haram remains to be seen, but the future does not look bright.

Notes

1 See Chapter 4.
2 Sahih Bukhari 5753, Sahih Muslim 60.
3 Shekau, A. 2015. 'Message to Paul Biya of Cameroon', in Kassim A. and Nwankpa, M. (eds.). *The Boko Haram Reader: From Nigerian Preachers to the Islamic State*. Oxford: Oxford University Press, pp. 357–360.
4 Jamaat Ansar al-Muslimin fi Bilad al-Sudan (Ansaru), "Allah is our Master". January 29, 2015. See Kassim, A. and Nwankpa, M. 2018. *The Boko Haram Reader: From Nigerian Preachers to the Islamic State*. Oxford and New York: Oxford University Press, pp. 375–376.
5 Shekau, A. 2016. 'Message to the world', in Kassim A. and Nwankpa, M. (eds.). *The Boko Haram Reader: From Nigerian Preachers to the Islamic State*. Oxford: Oxford University Press, pp. 441–444.

6 Nur, M. 2016. 'Expose: An Open letter to Abubakar Shekau', in Kassim A. and Nwankpa, M. (eds.). *The Boko Haram Reader: From Nigerian Preachers to the Islamic State*. Oxford: Oxford University Press, pp. 445–466.

7 Ibid.

8 Ibid.

9 Ibid.

10 Ibid.

11 Ibid.

12 Ibid.

13 Chari, M. 2016. 'Message from the Soldiers', in Kassim A. and Nwankpa, M. (eds.). *The Boko Haram Reader: From Nigerian Preachers to the Islamic State*. Oxford: Oxford University Press, pp. 467–470.

14 Ibid.

15 Shekau, A. 2016. 'Shekau Responds to his Critics', in Kassim A. and Nwankpa, M. (eds.). *The Boko Haram Reader: From Nigerian Preachers to the Islamic State*. Oxford: Oxford University Press, pp. 471–480.

16 Ibid.

17 Ibid.

7   Conclusion

This book has concerned itself with explaining the drivers of Boko Haram violence in northeastern Nigeria and beyond. The argument has been that there is no single factor that can explain what propelled Boko Haram into becoming the violent jihadist movement that it is today, but that, rather, a number of factors have to be taken into account. This is not to say that Boko Haram's progression to violence cannot be explained, nor that there are so many factors involved that they become useless in saying anything. Indeed, central to understanding the evolution of Boko Haram's violence is the movement's relationship to the history of Muslim west Africa, and the ways in which its leaders interpret and strategically frame that history to the movement's advantage. History, as Barkindo (2016) puts it, 'is a narration of the past in such a way as to make sense of the present.' Every chapter in this book has demonstrated how Boko Haram has drawn on history in order to legitimize its violence and to refute those who denounce the movement as un-Islamic.

To Boko Haram leaders, their movement is not an aberration or an innovation, but a legitimate force that is deeply rooted within a history of jihadist movements in the region, as well as to wider Islamic history. Whether Boko Haram leaders are denouncing corruption, espousing the dangers of western education, or calling for the implementation of an Islamic state in northern Nigeria with strict adherence to *shari'a*, the argument is grounded in the actions and examples of those who have gone before them, including the prophet Mohammad, Usman dan Fodio, and Ibn Abd al-Wahhab.

For all the attempts by Boko Haram to root itself within the context of what has gone before it, the movement is also a product of globalization and entrenched within the more immediate dynamics of 21st century west Africa. As MacEachern (2018: 183) argues,

> It is not a movement that could have developed a millennium or even a century ago, embedded as it is within a world of nation states and developing in a context of westernization, urbanism, and other Islamist

movements on other continents. At the same time, it is a movement anchored in a particular region of central Africa, and now, especially in the landscapes of plains, mountains, and lakeshores around Lake Chad. The histories of those landscapes and the cultural understandings of human actions that are generated by those histories account for some of BH's particular features.

This relationship to history, and in particular the pre-colonial history of the region climaxing in the establishment of a caliphate by Usman dan Fodio in 1804, is also powerfully linked to ideology – an ideology based on a supremacist form of Islam, which is aggressively hostile to notions of western education, democracy, and human rights, especially in the form of freedoms for women, sexual minorities, and non-Muslims in general. Indeed, this aspect was reflected in a speech given by Abubakar Shekau in June 2017:

> There is no way we Muslims in mosques and Christians in churches can work together. This has never happened before even during the lifetime of the apostles and prophets. If you are insisting on dialogue, we should have a situation where Muslims are ruling with Shari'a, and the non-Muslims agree to remain by the side without interference, then we can discuss their rights . . . But when the country is being run by constitution and democracy, such kind of dialogue cannot be possible.[1]

Not to miss the opportunity to further ground this within a historical reasoning, Shekau called on Nigerians to 'repent and to come and work for Islam, in accordance with the caliphate that was established by Usman dan Fodio, which is a caliphate built upon truth and belief in Allah.'[2] As such, in 2016, after the loss of their territorial gains, a key motivational objective of both factions of Boko Haram – JAS and ISWAP – is to see the establishment of an Islamic state in northern Nigeria. Their concept of carving out an Islamic state in northern Nigeria with political and military authority is based on historical precedence in the region, and one which has continued to resonate with Nigerian Islamists in contemporary times.

Boko Haram leaders were initially adept at identifying real social grievances in Nigeria and reframing these within an Islamist structure in order to mobilize segments of the population to their cause. At the moment of escalating violence in 2013, Boko Haram leaders were highlighting the huge levels of corruption in Nigeria and promising that under an Islamic order such injustices would be wiped out, just as they were during the time of dan Fodio. We know that this strategy was effective in garnering support for the movement, since the issue of corruption emerged as the most important factor in the analysis of a large-scale survey conducted in Nigeria in 2013. For example, the likelihood of believing that Boko Haram was a positive influence on Nigeria was significantly correlated with the perception that corruption is Nigeria's biggest problem. Belief that corruption was Nigeria's largest problem was associated with increased odds of seeing Boko Haram as a positive influence when compared with a respondent who believed that corruption was less important (Deckard & Pieri 2018: 381). This does not mean that all those people who believed corruption to be a major issue in Nigeria flocked to Boko Haram or supported the movement in its violence, but it did chime with interviews in Nigeria in which participants claimed that many people turned a blind eye to the movement's violence when it was first directed against the government.

While it is often acknowledged that Boko Haram initially operated as a movement oriented towards a transformation of society, it is evident even from its earliest moments, under the tutelage of Mohammad Yusuf, that there was at least some degree of willingness to employ violence in defense of its social agenda. Initial clashes were, however, localized around specific communities and events and, as such, are difficult to distinguish from other acts of violence, which are common occurrences in Nigeria. What is of importance, however, is that Yusuf developed rhetoric that became increasingly critical of, and hostile towards, the state, encouraging supporters to destroy certificates and diplomas of higher education (linked to any form of western schooling), as well as to band together to form policing groups and judicial systems that openly challenged the existing institutions of the state (Onuoha 2012). It is clear from such actions that Yusuf was keen from an early stage to establish a segregated form of governance, a parallel society within Nigeria for his own followers. Such attempts did not go unnoticed by the Nigerian state, which often pursued military responses to the issue rather than attempting to deal with the root causes of Yusuf's grievances (Cook 2014).

While Boko Haram's ideological underpinnings made it susceptible to violence, this outcome was not a foregone conclusion, and there is evidence of Mohammad Yusuf attempting to work with government officials in Borno State as a means of Islamizing the policies of that state. The issue with this stance, however, is that it assumes that attempts at engagement were genuine, which does not match with the discourse of the movement. Yusuf despised democracy, preached against the Nigerian constitution, and called for the implementation of an Islamic state at some point in the future. He worked with within the framework of politics in Borno so long as his demands were being met, but when the Islamization of policy did not go far enough (in his view), his discourse became increasingly more incendiary towards the government. This ultimately led to the circumstances in which Yusuf was extrajudicially executed and became the catalyst to tipping the movement towards a more definite violent approach.

A key driver of Boko Haram's violence is directly related to the way in which the Nigerian state interacted with Boko Haram – first through the extrajudicial killing of Mohammad Yusuf and other senior members, and then in the indiscriminate violence against the group by soldiers of the military's Joint Task Force (JTF). Indiscriminate violence by JTF soldiers, whether alleged or confirmed, substantiated a number of allegations against the Nigerian state put forth by Yusuf in his sermons and created a growing recruitment base of disaffected and unemployed youths. This allowed the movement to continuously regroup and threaten the Nigerian state despite sustained losses. Each major encounter between the military and Boko Haram members led to an evolution in the tactics used by Boko Haram. The 2009 military operations, for example, resulted in Boko Haram becoming far more inclined to utilize violence in order to achieve its goals. The movement completed its transformation from a largely non-violent and anti-establishment religious movement into a full-blown insurgency, with greater emphasis placed on the religious justification of violence against those who stood in its way.

This more violent approach contained the seeds that would ultimately lead the movement to its climax – the announcement of an Islamic state in Nigeria and an alliance with the terrorist movement of Abubakar al-Baghdadi, the self-proclaimed Caliph of the Islamic State of Iraq and Syria – but also contained the kernels of its fracturing. Abubakar Shekau, Boko Haram's leader following the death of Yusuf, veered evermore towards an unorthodox and extremist form of Islam, legitimizing the killing of all those who did not explicitly conform to the movement's worldview, including Muslims. This was an expression of *takfir* at its most intense, and one that backfired for Shekau, losing Boko Haram the support of many initial sympathizers, as well as the literal support of more orthodox Salafists within the ranks of the movement and amongst other international jihadist organizations such as the Islamic State and al Qaeda.

Shekau's uncompromising position with regards to the implementation of *takfir* led to the fracturing of Boko Haram and his demotion by the Islamic State from the leadership of ISWAP. A string of allegations was leveled against Shekau, many on the basis of a Salafist interpretation of Islam, which labeled him as an extremist, a 'khajirite,' and as having a shallow understanding of Islam. With his ejection from the leadership of ISWAP, Shekau reestablished his own branch of Boko Haram, reverting to the former name of JAS, and ever since the two factions have been in competition over resources, recruits, and operational space.

The fracturing of Boko Haram has important implications for any counter-terrorism and de-radicalization programs that may be established in Nigeria and the LCB. Understanding which faction fighters belong to is important and will affect the theological and ideological counter-narratives that are used in de-radicalization programs, especially for those who were aware of the arguments between Abu Musab al-Barnawi and Mamman Nur against Shekau and who actively picked a side. If Nigerian jihadists prove keen to adhere to Salafist principles, then the theological arguments against *takfir* emanating from al Qaeda, the Islamic State, and within ISWAP will do much to undermine Shekau's faction. Though the ideologies of Mamman Nur and ISWAP were considered to be somewhat more moderate, it is important to recognize that this moderation is relative to Shekau's faction, and as such ISWAP still has 'highly problematic understandings of *takfir* as well as *caliphacy* that need to be addressed in a de-radicalization program' (Zenn & Pieri 2017: 302).

The geo-political factors surrounding Boko Haram explain why the movement was able to metastasize in densely populated urban areas around the city of Maiduguri as well as more sparsely populated regions along the borders of Borno State. A primary factor in predicting the longevity of a given conflict often rests on geography, particularly mountainous and densely forested regions along the borders of countries (Buhaug et al. 2009; Tollefsen & Buhaug 2015). The Boko Haram conflict shares these geographic characteristics and has enabled the movement to engage the military and establish areas of territorial control at times of strength and to flee to the mountains, forests, or border regions in times of weakness (Onuoha 2012; Walker 2012).

This book has also demonstrated that it is unlikely that the drivers of Islamist violence in Nigeria and wider west Africa can be combated through a solely militaristic approach. While military operations, especially those in concert with the neighboring LCB countries, or through the use of mercenaries, can serve to hamper Boko Haram operationally, and in the long-term perhaps even crush the movement. If more such movements are not to re-develop in the future, non-military aspects of the conflict must also be addressed. Most pressing is the issue of corruption that has been identified as endemic to the Nigerian state and which is a factor that has mobilized people into action against the state. Without taking a comprehensive approach to the fight against Boko Haram, it is likely that Nigeria will remain in protracted conflicts with such groups for the long term.

Notes

1 Shekau, A. 2017. 'Speech on June 28'. www.vanguardngr.com/2017/06/kidnapped-ten-policewomen-says-shekau-new-video/ (accessed: December 27, 2018).
2 Ibid.

Bibliography

Abubakar, D. 2017. 'From Sectarianism to Terrorism in Northern Nigeria: A Closer Look at Boko Haram', in Varin, C. and Abubakar, D. (eds.). *Violent Non-State Actors in Africa: Terrorists, Rebels and Warlords*. London: Palgrave Macmillan.

Abusidiqu. 2014a. 'Boko Haram Installs "New Emir" in Bama, Prepares to Attack Maiduguri'. *Abusidiqu*. September 15. www.abusidiqu.com/boko-haram-installs-new-emir-bama-prepares-attack-maiduguri/ (accessed: December 20, 2018).

Abusidiqu. 2014b. 'Boko Haram Installs Another Emir in Dikwa after Doing Same in Bama, Sheu of Bama Threatens to March on Recapture Mission'. *Abusidiqu*. September 17. www.abusidiqu.com/boko-haram-installs-another-emir-in-dikwa-after-doing-same-in-bama-shehu-of-bama-threatens-to-march-on-recapture-mission/ (accessed: December 20, 2018).

Adeleye, R.A. 1971. *Power and Diplomacy in Northern Nigeria 1904–1906: The Sokoto Caliphate and its Enemies*. London: Longman.

Agbiboa, D. 2013. 'Why Boko Haram Exists: The Relative Deprivation Perspective'. *African Conflict and Peacebuilding Review*. 3: 144–157.

Aghedo, I. 2017. 'Old Wine in a New Bottle: Ideological and Operational Linkages Between Maitatsine and Boko Haram Revolts in Nigeria', in Hentz, J. and Solomon, H. (eds.). *Understanding Boko Haram: Terrorism and Insurgency in Africa*. London: Routledge.

Ajayi, O. 2017. 'Nigeria Recorded Over 40 Extra-Judicial Killings in 2016 – Rights Group'. *Vanguard*. August 20. www.vanguardngr.com/2017/08/nigeria-recorded-40-extra-judicial-killings-2016-rights-group/ (accessed: June 19, 2018).

Akhlaq, S. 2015. 'The Guise of the Sunni-Shiite use of Excommunication (Takfir) in the Middle East'. *Journal of South Asian and Middle Eastern Studies*. 38(4): 1–22.

Alkali, M. 1985. 'Some Contributions to the Study of the Pilgrimage Tradition in Nigeria'. *Annals of Borno*. II: 127–138.

Al-Risalah 4. 2017. https://azelin.files.wordpress.com/2017/01/al-risacc84lah-magazine-4.pdf (accessed: June 22, 2017).

Amnesty International. 2014. 'Nigeria: Government Knew of Planned Boko Haram Kidnapping but Failed to Act'. May 9. www.amnesty.org.uk/press-releases/nigeria-government-knew-planned-boko-haram-kidnapping-failed-act (accessed: June 13, 2018).

Amzat, A. 2017. 'Despite Decades of Funding, Literacy Level in the Northern States Remains Low'. *The Guardian*. July 24. https://guardian.ng/news/despite-decades-of-funding-literacy-level-in-the-northern-states-remains-low/ (accessed: June 13, 2018).

Ayandele, E. 1966. *Missionary Impact on Modern Nigeria: 1842–1914*. London: Longman.

Aziken, E. 2018. 'Week-long Ceasefire With Boko Haram Ended Yesterday'. March 26 Vanguard. https://www.vanguardngr.com/2018/03/week-long-ceasefire-boko-haram-ended-yesterday-fg/ (accessed 10 May 2019).

Baker, A. 2015. 'Nigeria's Military Quails When Faced with Boko Haram'. *Time*. February 10. http://time.com/3702849/nigerias-army-boko-haram/ (accessed: June 19, 2018).

Barkindo, A. 2016. 'Boko Haram Exploits History and Memory'. *Africa Research Institute*. October 4. www.africaresearchinstitute.org/newsite/publications/boko-haram-exploits-history-memory/ (accessed: October 11, 2018).

Barkindo, A. 2017. 'Tackling Boko Haram: Some Policy Ideas for Nigeria'. *Africa Research Institute*. February 23. www.africaresearchinstitute.org/newsite/blog/tackling-boko-haram-policy-ideas-nigeria/ (accessed: October 12, 2018).

Barkindo, A. 2018. 'Abubakr Shekau: Boko Haram's Underestimated Corporatist-Strategic Leader' in Zenn, J. (ed). Boko Haram Beyond the Headlines: Analyses of Africa's Enduring Insurgency. West Point: Combating Terrorism Center.

BBC News. 2004. 'Nigerians Crush Islamic Uprising'. September 22. http://news.bbc.co.uk/2/hi/africa/3679092.stm (accessed: June 20, 2018).

BBC News. 2009. 'Nigeria Sect Head Dies in Custody'. July 31. http://news.bbc.co.uk/2/hi/8177451.stm (accessed: June 22, 2018).

BBC News. 2018. 'Nigeria's Boko Haram Attacks in Numbers – As Lethal as Ever'. January 25. www.bbc.com/news/world-africa-42735414 (accessed: October 11, 2018).

Bello, A. 1962. *My Life*. Cambridge: Cambridge University Press.

Bloom, M. and Matfess, H. 2016. 'Women as Symbols and Swords in Boko Haram's Terror'. *Peace*. 6(1): 105–121.

Boyle, J. 2009. 'Nigeria's "Taliban" Enigma"'. *BBC News*. July 31. http://news.bbc.co.uk/2/hi/8172270.stm (accessed: June 14, 2018).

Bradford, E. and Wilson, M. 2013. 'When Terrorists Attack Schools: An Explanatory Analysis of Attacks on Educational Institutions'. *Journal of Police and Criminal Psychology*. 28: 127–138.

Brenner, L. 1979. 'Muhammad Al-Amin al-Kanemi and Religion and Politics in Bornu', in Willis, J. (ed.). *Studies in West African Islamic History: The Cultivators of Islam*. Vol. 1. London: Frank Cass.

Brigaglia, A. 2018. '"Slicing the Tumor": The History of Global Jihad in Nigeria, as Narrated by the Islamic State'. *Politics and Religion*. 2(12): 199–224.

Bryson, R. and Bukarti, A. 2018. 'Boko Haram's Split on Women in Combat'. *Tony Blair Institute for Global Change*. September 17. https://institute.global/insight/co-existence/boko-harams-split-women-combat (accessed: January 27, 2019).

Buhari, M. 2015. 'Muhammadu Buhari: We Will Stop Boko Haram'. *New York Times*. April 14.

Buhari, M. 2016. 'Speech at the Anti-Corruption Summit, London'. May 11. www. opengovpartnership.org/stories/full-text-of-buhari-s-speech-anti-corruption-summit-london (accessed: June 18, 2018).

Buhaug, H., Gates, S. and Lujala, P. 2009. 'Geography, Rebel Capability, and the Duration of Civil Conflict'. *Journal of Conflict Resolution*. 53(4): 544–569.

Campbell, J. 2014. *Nigeria Security Tracker Monthly Update*. September. www. cfr.org/blog/nigeria-security-tracker-weekly-update-september-13-september-19 (accessed: December 27, 2018).

Cohen, R. 1967. *The Kanuri of Bornu*. New York: Holt, Rinehart and Winston.

Comolli, V. 2015. Boko Haram: Nigeria's Islamist Insurgency. London: Hurst.

Coles, C. and Mack, B. 1991. *Hausa Women in the Twentieth Century*. Madison: University of Wisconsin Press.

Cook, D. 2014. 'Boko Haram: A New Islamic State in Nigeria'. *James A. Baker III Institute for Public Policy*. www.bakerinstitute.org/media/files/files/5f1f63c4/BI-pub-BokoHaram-121114.pdf (accessed: October 10, 2018).

Crowder, M. 1962. *A Short History of Nigeria*. New York: Frederick A. Prager.

D'Amato, S. (2018) 'Terrorists Going Transnational: Rethinking the Role of States in the Case of AQIM and Boko Haram'. *Critical Studies on Terrorism*. 11(1): 151–172.

Danmole, H.O. 1996. 'Religion and the Colonial State', in Elaigwu, J. and Uzoigwe, G. (eds.). *Foundations of Nigerian Federalism 1900–1960*. Abuja: National Council on Intergovernmental Affairs.

Deckard, N., Barkindo, A. and Jacobson, D. 2015. 'Religiosity and Rebellion in Nigeria: Considering Boko Haram in the Radical Tradition'. *Studies in Conflict & Terrorism*. 38(7): 238–510.

Deckard, N. and Pieri, Z. 2017. 'The Implications of Endemic Corruption for State Legitimacy in Developing Nations: An Empirical Exploration of the Nigerian Case'. *International Journal of Politics, Culture, and Society*. 30(4): 369–384.

The Economist. 2007. 'Sharia Lite: Moderation from Nigeria's Islamist State Governments'. *The Economist*. February 1. www.economist.com/node/8636164 (accessed: December 20, 2018).

The Economist. 2010. 'Nigeria's Religious Police Out on Patrol'. *The Economist*. June 11. www.economist.com/node/16311947?zid=304&ah=e5690753dc78ce91 909083042ad12e30 (accessed: December 20, 2018).

The Economist. 2018. 'Boko Haram is Becoming Even More Extreme'. *The Economist*. November 22. www.economist.com/middle-east-and-africa/2018/11/24/ boko-haram-is-becoming-even-more-extreme (accessed: December 1, 2018).

Eikmeier, D. 2007. 'Qutbsim: An Ideology of Islamic-fascism'. *Parameters: U.S. Army War College Journal*. (Spring): 85–97.

Elechi, O. 2003. 'Extra-Judicial Killings in Nigeria – The Case of Afikpo Town'. 17th International Conference of the International Society for the Reform of Criminal Law. The Hague, Netherlands, August 24–28.

Eltantawi, S. 2017. *Shari'ah on Trial: Northern Nigeria's Islamic Revolution*. Oakland: University of California Press.

Falola, T. and Heaton, M. 2008. *A History of Nigeria*. Cambridge: Cambridge University Press.

Falola, T., Uhomoibhi, A., Mahdi, A. and Anyanwu, U. 2007. *History of Nigeria 2: Nigeria in the Nineteenth Century*. Lagos: Longman Nigeria.

Hansen, W. 2017. 'Boko Haram: Religious Radicalism and Insurrection in Northern Nigeria'. *Journal of Asian and African Studies*. 52(4): 551–569.

Haruna, A. 2018a. 'Boko Haram: "I am Tired of This Calamity," Shekau Says in New Video'. *Premium Times*. February 7. www.premiumtimesng.com/news/headlines/257876-boko-haram-i-tired-calamity-shekau-says-new-video.html (accessed: December 23, 2018).

Haruna, A. 2018b. 'Boko Haram Leader Shekau Mocks Chibok Girls Parents, Says We're In-laws'. *Premium Times*. January 16. www.premiumtimesng.com/news/headlines/255716-boko-haram-leader-shekau-mocks-chibok-girls-parents-says-laws.html (accessed: December 23, 2018).

Hassan, I. and Pieri, Z. 2018. "The Rise and Risks of Nigeria's Civilian Joint Task Force: Implications for Post-Conflict Recovery in Northeastern Nigeria", in Zenn, Jacob (ed.), *Boko Haram Beyond the Headlines: Analyses of Africa's Enduring Conflict*, West Point: Combating Terrorism Center. pp. 74-86.

Hegghammer, T. 2009. 'Jihadi-Salafis or Revolutionaries? On Religion and Politics in the Study of Militant Islamism', in Meijer, R. (ed.). *Global Salafism: Islam's New Religious Movement*. London and New York: Hurst & Company.

Hegghammer, T. (ed.). 2017. *Jihadi Culture: The Art and Social Practices of Militant Islamists*. Cambridge: Cambridge University Press.

Hentz, J. and Solomon, H. (eds.). 2017. Understanding Boko Haram: Terrorism and Insurgency in Africa. New York: Routledge.

Higazi, A., Kendhammer, B., Mohammed, K., Perouse de Montclos, M. and Thurston, A. 2018. 'A Response to Jacob Zenn on Boko Haram and al-Qa'ida'. *Perspectives on Terrorism*. 12(2): 200–210.

Hiskett, M. 1973. *The Sword of Truth: The Life and Times of The Shehu Usman Dan Fodio*. New York: Oxford University Press.

Hiskett, M. 1984. *The Development of Islam in West Africa*. London and New York: Longman.

Hoechner, Hannah. 2014. 'Traditional Quranic Students (almajirai) in Nigeria: Fair Game for Unfair Accusations?' in Persouse de Montclos, M. (ed.) Boko Haram: Islamism, Politics, Security and the State in Nigeria.

Human Rights Watch. 2012. 'Spiraling Violence: Boko Haram Attacks and Security Force Abuses in Nigeria'. *Human Rights Watch*. October 11. www.hrw.org/report/2012/10/11/spiraling-violence/boko-haram-attacks-and-security-force-abuses-nigeria (accessed: October 10, 2018).

Human Rights Watch. 2015. 'Dispatches: What Really Happened in Baga, Nigeria?'. *Human Rights Watch*. January 14. www.hrw.org/news/2015/01/14/dispatches-what-really-happened-baga-nigeria (accessed: December 15, 2018).

Human Rights Watch. 2016. 'They Set the Classroom on Fire: Attacks on Education in Northeast Nigeria'. April 11. www.hrw.org/report/2016/04/11/they-set-classrooms-fire/attacks-education-northeast-nigeria (accessed: June 13, 2018).

Ibraheem, S. 2009. The African Caliphate: The Life, Works and Teaching of Shaykh Usman Dan Fodio (1754–1817) London: The Diwan Press.

Idris, H. and Sawab, I. 2018. 'Factional Boko Haram Leader Mamman Nur Killed by Own Fighters'. *Daily Trust*. September 14. www.dailytrust.com.

ng/factional-boko-haram-leader-mamman-nur-killed-by-own-fighters.html (accessed: December 19, 2018).

International Crisis Group. 2014. 'Curbing Violence in Nigeria (II): The Boko Haram Insurgency'. *International Crisis Group Africa Report # 216*. April 3. www.ecoi.net/file_upload/1226_1396951718_216-curbing-violence-in-nigeria-ii-the-boko-haram-insurgency.pdf (accessed: June 22, 2017).

Isa, M. 2010. 'Militant Islamist Groups in Northern Nigeria', in Okumu, W. and Ikelegbe, A. (eds.). *Militias, Rebels and Islamist Militants: Human Security and State Crises in Africa*. Pretoria: Institute for Security Studies.

Isichei, E. 1977. *History of West Africa Since 1800*. New York: Africana Publishing Company.

ISWAP. 2018. *Slicing the Tumor*. Trans. Al-Tamimi, A.J. August 5. www.aymennjawad.org/21467/the-islamic-state-west-africa-province-vs-abu (accessed: August 10, 2018).

Johnston, H.A.S. 1967. *The Fulani Empire of Sokoto*. Oxford and London: Oxford University Press.

Johnston, H.A.S. and Muffet, D.J.M. 1973. *Denham in Bornu: An Account of the Exploration of Bornu Between 1823 & 1825 by Major Dixon Denham, Dr. Oudney and Commander Hugh Clapperton and of Their Dealings with Sheikh Muhammad El Amin El Kanemi*. New York: Duquesne University Press.

Kassim, A. and Nwankpa, M. (eds.). 2018. *The Boko Haram Reader: From Nigerian Preachers to the Islamic State*. Oxford and New York: Oxford University Press.

Kendhammer, B. 2013. 'The Sharia Controversy in Northern Nigeria and the Politics of Islamic Law in New Uncertain Democracies'. *Comparative Politics*. 45(3): 291–311.

Kollere, A. 2007. 'Nigeria: Maiduguri 1907–2007 – A Century of Excellence'. *Daily Trust*. June 3. http://allafrica.com/stories/200706041403.html (accessed: March 13, 2014).

Last, M. 1967. The Sokoto Caliphate. Bristol: Longmans, Green and Co.

Last, M. 2014. 'From Dissent to Dissidence: The Genesis and Development of Reformist Islamic Groups in Northern Nigeria', in Mustapha, A. (ed.). *Sects & Social Disorder: Muslim Identities & Conflict in Northern Nigeria*. London: James Currey.

Last, M. and Al-Hajj, M. 1965. 'Attempts at Defining a Muslim in 19th Century Hausaland and Bornu'. *Journal of the Historical Society of Nigeria*. 3(2): 231–240.

Leithead, A. and Hegarty, S. 2017. 'The Fate of the Chibok Girls'. *BBC News*. May 19. www.bbc.co.uk/news/resources/idt-sh/chibok_girls (accessed: June 13, 2018).

Lugard, F. 1904. *Political Memoranda*. MSS Lugard 55/2 ff. 1–114.

MacEachern, S. 2018. *Searching for Boko Haram: A History of Violence in Central Africa*. Oxford: Oxford University Press.

Macpherson, N., Arua, M. and Out, M. 2018. 'The Use of Women and Children in Suicide Bombing by the Boko Haram Terrorist Group in Nigeria'. *Aggression and Violent Behavior*. 42: 35–42.

Mahmood, O. 2018. 'An Internal Shift Points to a Growing Threat in the Lake Chad Region'. *Institute for Security Studies*. November 28. https://issafrica.org/iss-today/is-islamic-state-in-west-africa-becoming-more-hardline (accessed: December 19, 2018).

Mark, M. 2012. 'Boko Haram Vows to Fight Until Nigeria Establishes Sharia law'. *The Guardian*. January 27. http://gu.com/p/354ax (accessed: December 26, 2018).

McCants, W. 2015. 'The Believer: How an Introvert with a Passion for Religion and Soccer Became Abu Bakar al-Baghdadi Leader of the Islamic State'. *Brookings Institution*. September 1. http://csweb.brookings.edu/content/research/essays/2015/thebeliever.html (accessed: December 13, 2018).

McClean, R. 2016. 'Boko Haram Releases Video Appearing to Show Chibok Schoolgirls'. *The Guardian*. August 14. www.theguardian.com/world/2016/aug/14/boko-haram-releases-video-chibok-schoolgirls-nigeria (accessed: December 23, 2018).

Mejia-Johnson, A. and Piracha, S. 2012. *Recording a Revolution: A Story of Music, Religion and Identity*. A film produced by O'Brien, S. and Villalon, L. The Centre for African Studies, University of Florida.

Muhammad, K. 2014. 'The Message and Methods of Boko Haram', in Perouse de Montclos, M. (ed.). *Boko Haram: Islamism, Politics, Security and the State in Nigeria*. Leiden and Ibadan: African Studies Centre and French Institute for Research in Africa.

Murray, J. 2004. 'Interpol Trails Yobe Taliban Leader to Saudi'. *The Punch*. January 29.

Muscati, S. and Hassan, T. 2015. 'Anatomy of a Boko Haram Massacre'. *Foreign Policy*. June 10. https://foreignpolicy.com/2015/06/10/anatomy-of-a-boko-haram-massacre/ (accessed: December 14, 2018).

Mustapha, A. (ed.). 2014. *Sects & Social Disorder: Muslim Identities & Conflict in Northern Nigeria*. London: James Currey.

Newman, P. 2013. The etymology of Hausa boko. Mega-Chad Miscellaneous Publications, pp. 1-13.

Niven, C.R. 1949. Report on, *Bornu Province: Northern Territories – Nigeria 1949*. CO 1018/38.

Nnam, M., Aru, M., Otu, M. 2018. 'The Use of Women and Children in Suicide Bombing by the Boko Haram Terrorist Group in Nigeria'. Aggression and Violent Behavior. 42(5): 35-42.

Nur-Awaleh, M. 2006. 'The Fulani Jihad and the Rise to Power in Hausaland in the 19th Century', in Sarr, A. (ed.). *The Histories, Languages and Cultures of West Africa: Interdisciplinary Essays*. New York: Edwin Mellen Press.

OCHA. 2017. 'North-East Nigeria Humanitarian Situation Update'. *United Nations Office for the Coordination of Human Affairs*. October 20. https://reliefweb.int/sites/reliefweb.int/files/resources/20102017_ocha_nga_ne_sitrep_no_sept_2017.pdf (accessed: December 27, 2018).

Ofongo, O. 2016. 'The Boko Haram Insurgency in Nigeria: What Could Have Been the Precursors?' *Journal for Deradicalization*. 7(2): 145–163.

Ogundipe, S. 2018. 'Metele Boko Haram Attack: Soldiers' Death Toll Rises to 118; Over 150 Missing'. *Premium Times*. November 24. www.premiumtimesng.com/news/headlines/297343-metele-boko-haram-attack-soldiers-death-toll-rises-to-118-over-150-missing.html (accessed: December 19, 2018).

Ojo, O.E. (2010). 'Boko Haram: Nigeria's Extra-Judicial State'. *Journal of Sustainable Development in Africa*. 12(2): 45–62.

Olaniyan, A. 2017. 'Feminization of Terror: Boko Haram and Female Suicide Bombers in Nigeria'. *Politics, International Relations and Law*. June 6. https://

think.iafor.org/feminization-of-terror-boko-haram-and-female-suicide-bombers-in-nigeria/ (accessed: December 27, 2018).

Onuoha, F. 2012. 'Boko Haram: Nigeria's Extremist Islamic Sect'. *Al Jazeera*. February 29. http://studies.aljazeera.net/mritems/Documents/2012/2/29/20122 29113341793734BOKO%20HARAM%20NIGERIAS%20EXTREMIST%20 ISLAMIC%20SECT.pdf (accessed: December 26, 2018).

Oriola, T. and Akinola, O. 2018. 'Ideational Dimensions of the Boko Haram Phenomenon'. *Studies in Conflict and Terrorism*. 41(8): 595–618.

Oropo, K. 2004. 'How Talibans Recruit, Operate Nationwide'. *The Guardian*. January 18. www.africafiles.org/article.asp?ID=4235 (accessed: June 22, 2017).

Pantucci, R. and Jesperson, S. 2015. *From Boko Haram to Ansaru: The Evolution of Nigerian Jihad*. London: Royal United Services Institute.

Pearson, E. 2018. 'Wilayat Shahidat: Boko Haram, the Islamic State, and the Question of the Female Suicide Bomber', in Zenn, J. (ed.). *Boko Haram Beyond the Headlines: Analyses of Africa's Enduring Insurgency*. West Point: Combating Terrorism Center.

Pereira, C. 2018. 'Beyond the Spectacular: Contextualizing Gender Relations in the Wake of the Boko Haram Insurgency'. *Meridians*. 17(2): 246–268.

Perouse de Montclos, M. 2014. Boko Haram: Islamism, Politics, Security and the State in Nigeria. Leiden: Africa Studies Centre.

Perouse de Montclos, M. 2017. 'Boko Haram: A Jihadist Enigma in Nigeria', in Hentz, J. and Solomon, H. (eds.). *Understanding Boko Haram: Terrorism and Insurgency in Africa*. London: Routledge.

Pieri, Z. 2015. *Tablighi Jamaat and the Quest for the London Mega Mosque: Continuity and Change*. London and New York: Palgrave Macmillan.

Pieri, Z. and Barkindo, A. 2016. 'Muslims in Nigeria: Between Challenge and Opportunity', in Mason, R. (ed.). *Muslim Minority – State Relations: Violence, Integration and Policy*. London and New York: Palgrave Macmillan.

Pieri, Z. and Zenn, J. 2016. 'The Boko Haram Paradox: Ethnicity, Religion, and Historical Memory in Pursuit of a Caliphate'. *African Security*. 9(1): 66–88.

Pieri, Z. and Zenn, J. 2017. 'The Boko Haram Paradox: Ethnicity, Religion, and Historical Memory in Pursuit of a Caliphate', in Hentz, J. and Solomon, H. (eds.). *Understanding Boko Haram: Terrorism and Insurgency in Africa*. New York and London: Routledge.

Pieri, Z. and Zenn, J. 2018. 'Under the Black Flag in Borno: Experiences of Foot soldiers and Civilians in Boko Haram's "caliphate" '. *Journal of Modern African Studies*. 56(4): 645–672.

Pieri, Z.; Woodward, M. Yahya, M.; Hassan, I.; Rohmaniyah, I.. 2014. "Commanding Good and Prohibiting Evil in Contemporary Islam: Cases from Britain, Nigeria and Southeast Asia." *Contemporary Islam*, 8:1, pp. 37-55.

Rashid, A. 2017. 'Documents of Advice and Sharia Instruction to The Fighters in Nigeria'. April 13, but dated to before Usama bin Laden's death in May 2011. https://azelin.files.wordpress.com/2017/04/shaykh-abucc84-al-hcca3asan-rashicc84d-22sharicc84ah-advice-and-guidance-for-the-mujacc84hidicc84n-of-nigeria22.pdf (accessed: June 22, 2017).

Sahara Reporters. 2018a. 'Boko Haram's Leader Mamman Nur Killed by His Closet Lieutenants for Releasing Dapchi Girls'. *Sahara Reporters*. September 14. http://saharareporters.com/2018/09/14/boko-haram-leader-mamman-nur-killed-his-closest-lieutenants-releasing-dapchi-girls (accessed: December 1, 2018).

Sahara Reporters. 2018b. 'Salkida Says New Information from Boko Haram Indicates 30 Chibok Girls in Custody Still Alive'. *Sahara Reporters*. April 18. http://saharareporters.com/2018/04/18/salkida-says-new-information-boko-haram-indicates-30-chibok-girls-custody-still-alive (accessed: June 15, 2018).

Schultze, A. 1913. *The Sultanate of Bornu*. Trans. Benton, P.A. London and New York: Humphrey Milford and Oxford University Press.

Scott, P.H.G. 1952. A Survey of Islam in Northern Nigeria in 1952. Kaduna: Government Printer.

Serano, R. and Pieri, Z. 2014. 'By the Numbers: The Nigerian State's Efforts to Counter Boko Haram', in Perouse de Montclos, M. (ed.). *Boko Haram: Islamism, Politics, Security and the State in Nigeria*. Leiden and Ibadan: African Studies Centre and French Institute for Research in Africa.

Shekau, A. 2009. 'This is Our Creed' in Kassim, A. and Nwankpa, N. (eds.). 2018. The Boko Haram Reader: From Nigerian Preachers to the Islamic State. Oxford: Oxford University Press. pp. 139-146.

Shekau, A. 2014. 'Message About the Chibok Girls' in Kassim, A. and Nwankpa, M. (eds.). The Boko Haram Reader: From Nigerian Preachers to the Islamic State. Oxford: Oxford University Press, pp. 311-317.

Shekau, A. 2014. 'Message About the Chibok Girls' in Kassim, A. and Nwankpa, M. (eds.). The Boko Haram Reader: From Nigerian Preachers to the Islamic State. Oxford: Oxford University Press, pp. 321-326.

Shekau, A. 2014. 'Message About the Chibok Girls' in Kassim, A. and Nwankpa, M. (eds.). The Boko Haram Reader: From Nigerian Preachers to the Islamic State. Oxford: Oxford University Press, pp. 311-318.

Shekau, A. 2014. 'Message to the Ummah'. in Kassim, A. and Nwankpa, M. (eds). The Boko Haram Reader: From Nigerian Preachers to the Islamic State . Oxford: Oxford University Press, pp. 301-309.

Sonn, T. and Farrar, A. 2010. *'Kharijites'. Oxford Bibliographies*. Oxford: Oxford University Press.

START. 2014. 'Boko Haram Recent Attacks: Background Report'. *National Consortium for the Study of Terrorism and Responses to Terrorism*. May. www.start.umd.edu/pubs/STARTBackgroundReport_BokoHaramRecentAttacks_May2014_0.pdf (accessed: June 13, 2018).

Suliman, I. 2009. *The African Caliphate: The Life, Works and Teaching of Shaykh Usman Dan Fodio (1754–1817)*. London: The Diwan Press.

Thurston, A. 2016. 'The Disease is Unbelief": Boko Haram's Religious & Political Worldview'. *The Brookings Institution*. Analysis Paper January 22.

Thurston, A. 2018. 'Five Myths About Boko Haram'. *Lawfare*. January 14. www.lawfareblog.com/five-myths-about-boko-haram (accessed: November 30, 2018).

Tibenderana, P. 1983. 'The Emirs and the Spread of Western Education in Northern Nigeria, 1910-1946'. *The Journal of African History* 24(4): pp. 517–34.

Tollefsen, A. and Buhaug, H. 2015. 'Insurgency and Inaccessibility'. *International Studies Review*. 17(1): 6–25.

Toromade, S. 2018. 'Presidency says Boko Haram Remains "Technically Defeated" Despite Metele Attack'. *Pulse*. November 26. www.pulse.ng/news/local/presidency-says-boko-haram-remains-technically-defeated-despite-metele-attack/d4l6sxy (accessed: January 17, 2019).

Transparency International. 2018. 'Corruption Perceptions Index 2017'. February 21. www.transparency.org/news/feature/corruption_perceptions_index_2017 (accessed: October 11, 2018).

Trimingham, J.S. 1959. *Islam in West Africa*. Oxford: Clarendon Press.

Umar, S. 2009. *Press Release*. August 9. Vanguard. www.vanguardngr.com/2009/08/boko-haram-ressurects-declares-total-jihad/ (accessed: June 22, 2017).

UNDP. 2017. 'Journey to Extremism in Africa: Drivers, Incentives and the Tipping Point for Recruitment'. *United Nations Development Program*. http://journey-to-extremism.undp.org/content/downloads/UNDP-JourneyToExtremism-report-2017-english.pdf (accessed: October 11, 2018).

Utietiang, B. 2016. 'President Muhammadu Buhari's Boko Haram Deluison'. *Huffington Post*. March 18. www.huffingtonpost.com/bekeh-utietiang/president-muhammadu-boko-haram-delusion_b_9482338.html (accessed: January 17, 2019).

Varin, C. 2016. *Boko Haram and the War on Terror*. Santa Barbara, CA: Praeger.

VerEecke, C. 1985. 'Towards an Ethnohistory of the Adamawa Fulbe in the 19th Century'. *Annals of Borno*. 2: 163–179.

VOA. 2017a. 'Boko Haram: Terror Unmasked'. *Voice of America*. February. https://projects.voanews.com/boko-haram-terror-unmasked/ (accessed: December 27, 2018).

VOA. 2017b. 'Boko Haram: Journey from Evil'. November 10. https://projects.voanews.com/boko-haram-journey-from-evil/ (accessed: December 27, 2018).

Walker, A. 'What is Boko Haram?' United States Institute of Peace. Special Report 308.

Walker, A. 2016. *'Eat the Heart of the Infidel': The Harrowing of Nigeria and the Rise of Boko Haram*. London: Hurst & Company.

Warner, J. and Matfess, H. 2017. *Exploding Stereotypes: The Unexpected Operational and Demographic Characteristics of Boko Haram's Suicide Bombers*. West Point: Combating Terrorism Center.

Webster, J.B. and Bohen, A.A. 1970. *History of West Africa: The Revolutionary Years – 1815 to Independence*. New York and Washington: Praeger.

Wiktorowicz, Q. 2006. 'Anatomy of the Salafi Movement'. *Studies in Conflict and Terrorism*. 29(3): 207–239.

Willis, J. (ed.). (1979). *Studies in West African Islamic History: The Cultivators of Islam*. Vol 1. London: Frank Cass.

Wood, G. 2015. 'What ISIS Really Wants'. *The Atlantic*. March. www.theatlantic.com/magazine/archive/2015/03/what-isis-really-wants/384980/ (accessed: June 22, 2017).

Yusuf, B. 1991. 'Hausa-Fulani-Women: The State of the Struggle', in Coles, C. and Mack, B. (eds.). *Hausa Women in the Twentieth Century*. Madison: University of Wisconsin Press.

Yusuf, M. 2007. *Tarihin Musulmai [History of Muslims]*. Trans. Atta Barkindo. www.youtube.com/watch?v=eUQYNucjqUE (accessed: June 22, 2017).

Zenn, J. (ed.). 2018e. *Boko Haram Beyond the Headlines: Analyses of Africa's Enduring Conflict*, West Point: Combating Terrorism Center.

Zenn, J. 2018b. 'Is Boko Haram's Notorious Leader About to Return from the Dead Again?' *African Arguments*. December 10. https://africanarguments.org/2018/12/10/boko-haram-notorious-leader-shekau-return-from-dead-again/ (accessed: December 15, 2018).

Zenn, J. 2018c. 'Competing Ideologies at Play in Boko Haram's Return of Dapchi Girls'. *Council on Foreign Relations*. April 4. www.cfr.org/blog/competing-ideologies-play-boko-harams-return-dapchi-girls (accessed: November 27, 2018).

Zenn, J. 2018d. 'A Primer on Boko Haram Sources and Three Heuristics on al-Qaida and Boko Haram in Response to Adam Higazi, Brandon Kendhammer, Kyari Mohammed, Marc-Antoine Perouse de Montclos, and Alex Thurston'. *Perspectives on Terrorism*. 12(3): 74–91.

Zenn, J. 2018a. 'Boko Haram's Conquest for the Caliphate: How al Qaeda Helped Islamic State Acquire Territory'. *Studies in Conflict and Terrorism*. DOI: 10.1080/1057610X.2018.1442141.

Zenn, J. and Pearson, E. 2014. 'Women, Gender and the Evolving Tactics of Boko Haram'. *Journal for Terrorism Research*. 5(1): 46–57.

Zenn, J. and Pieri, Z. 2017. 'How Much Takfir Is too Much Takfir? The Evolution of Boko Haram's Factionalization'. *Journal for Deradicalization*. 11(3): 281–308.

Zimet, P. 2017. 'Boko Haram's Evolving Relationship with Al-Qaeda'. *Generva Centre for Security Policy*. September 13. www.gcsp.ch/News-Knowledge/Global-insight/Boko-Haram-s-Evolving-Relationship-With-al-Qaeda (accessed: October 30, 2018).

Index

Nur, Mamman 64, 75, 76, 79, 86n6, 87, 93, 98
Nwankpa, M. 6

Obama, Michelle 61
Operation Flush 42

Pearson, Elizabeth 59
Pereira, Charmaine 64
personal agency of youth 3
Pieri, Zacharias P. 74, 94
political context of post-1999 electoral competition 3
polytheists 22
poverty and inequality 3
pre-modern "globalization" 23
pristine age of Islam 35
prophet Mohammad 12, 19, 20, 35, 61, 80, 89
punishments 70
puritanism 25

Qadiriyya 24
Qaqa, Abu 59
Qur'an 16, 33, 35–38, 41, 55, 60–61, 89, 91, 98
Qur'anic schools 16, 19, 55, 61
Qutb, Sayyid 89

Raji, Muhammad dan 24
reformist movements 12
religious doctrines 3
revivalist Islam 27n4
rogue Islamist movement 11
Royal Niger Company 23, 51

Salafi-jihadism 2, 7, 28
Salafi-jihadist movements 98
Salafist Group for Preaching and Combat 92
Salafist strand of Islam 4
Salkida, Ahmad 65
Schultze, A. 12
Scott, P.H.G. 55
Shari'a Court of Appeal 83
shari'a law 2, 11–12, 35, 70, 82, 91
Shehu of Bornu 14
Shekau 90–92
Shekau, Abubakar 1, 4, 28, 44, 48, 56, 63, 69, 86n1, 86n2, 87, 103n6; oath

75; western education, movements against 49
Sheriff, Modu 38, 40
Shettima, Adamu 35
Shi'a Islamic Movement 33
Slicing the Tumor 6, 33, 36, 72, 90, 91, 93
social grievances 2
societal re-orientation program 84
Sokoto Caliphate 2, 7, 16, 18, 50
Sokoto jihad 13
southeastern Niger 11
Southern Protectorate of Nigeria 13
state corruption 2
Sudan 14
Sudanic Africa 52
Sufi brotherhood 24
Sufi mysticism 12
Sufi principles 12
suicide bombings 72; in Cameroon 74
Sultan of Borno 22
sunna 35
Sunni Group for Proselytization and Jihad (JAS) 4
Sunni Muslims 41

Tablighi Jamaat 2, 50
taghut 40
Ta'ifa Mansura mosque 36
takfir 5, 8, 16, 88–92, 100
takfiri jihadist group 28, 34
takfiring 72
takfirism 2
Talib, Ali ibn 89
Taliban in Afghanistan 50
Taymiyyah, Ibn 40, 47n2
Thurston, A. 3
Tibenderana, Peter 54
Timbuktu, Mali 73
Transparency International 29
Tugwell, Bishop 53

Umar, al-Haji 12
Umar, Ibn 89
Umar, Sani 4, 9n1, 27n5, 44
Umar, Saniu 18
Umar, Sheikh Jibril 16
urban sins 84

violence 28–29; Mohammad Yusuf and genesis of Boko Haram 33–36;

For Product Safety Concerns and Information please contact our EU
representative GPSR@taylorandfrancis.com
Taylor & Francis Verlag GmbH, Kaufingerstraße 24, 80331 München, Germany